PROPERTY OF
Chenango Co. Catholic Charities

D0255534

caren adams and jenni

Crime Victims/Witness Assistance Program
19 Prospect Street
Norwich, N.Y. 13815
(607) 334-3532
24-Hour Availability

NO

MORE

SECRETS

protecting your child from sexual assault

Impact 🟦 *Publishers*
POST OFFICE BOX 1094
SAN LUIS OBISPO, CALIFORNIA 93406

PROPERTY OF
Chenango Co. Catholic Charities

Copyright © 1981

by Caren Adams and Jennifer Fay

All rights reserved under International and Pan-American Copyright Conventions. Except as noted below, no part of this book may be reproduced, stored in a retrieval system, or transmitted in any form or by any means, electronic, mechanical, photocopying, recording or otherwise, without express written permission of the authors or publisher. Brief quotations are permitted in critical reviews. The "Action Suggestions for Parents," page 87, may be reproduced without further permission, so long as its credit line is included on each and every copy thereof.

Some of the material in this book is from the booklet "He Told Me Not to Tell," copyright © 1979, King County Rape Relief, Renton, WA 98055.

PUBLISHER'S NOTE

This publication is designed to provide accurate and authoritative information in regard to the subject matter covered. It is sold with the understanding that the publisher is not engaged in rendering psychological, medical, or other professional services. If expert assistance or counseling is needed, the services of a competent professional should be sought.

Library of Congress Cataloging in Publication data:

Adams, Caren, 1946-
    No more secrets.

    Bibliography: p.
    1. Child molesting--Prevention. 2.Pedophilia--
Prevention. I. Fay, Jennifer, 1949-   . II. Title.
HQ71.A37   649'.65   81-3931
ISBN 0-915166-24-0   AACR2

Printed in the United States of America   Eighth Printing, January, 1985

Published by   *Impact* 🐢 *Publishers*
                    POST OFFICE BOX 1094
            SAN LUIS OBISPO, CALIFORNIA 93406

Acknowledgements

Most of the information in this book grew from our work on the staff of King County Rape Relief (KCRR) in Washington State. Parents whose children had been assaulted and parents concerned about that possibility were uncertain about how to talk to their children about sexual assault. There was nothing written to help. That gap was filled by a booklet for parents of children up to 12 years old produced by KCRR called "He Told Me Not To Tell". The practical suggestions from that booklet are extended here.

We are grateful to the original founders of King County Rape Relief the Renton, Washington chapter of the National Organization for Women, and all of the volunteers at KCRR who have contributed time, caring, and late night hours to be sure that people no longer have to face this crisis alone. We want to thank the many parents who were willing to share their experiences with us. To those people who said we have something to say and helped us say it, thank you. A special mention goes to Billie Jo Flerchinger, Tina Bierma, Debbie Waldher, Annie Bruck, Leo Baldyga, Suzie Till, Lois Fay, Carol Lick, Florence Rose, Michele Pomarico, and Pat Rittenhouse.

We would also like to thank our husbands Robbie and Herb for their support. We especially appreciate Robbie's many hours of help in preparing the manuscript. To Toby, Piper and Ginevra, who let us practice, "you are in here."

C.A.

Renton, Washington

J.F.

January 1981

Table of Contents

To all those children who will know what to do.

Chapter 1
No Horror Stories

Introduction

> *"My seven year old daughter was watching TV with her 25 year old Uncle Pete. He was babysitting her while we were at the movies. Lisa is an active child who really enjoys wrestling with Pete. That night, Lisa and Pete had a good time wrestling together during the commercials, but things got out of hand. Pete asked Lisa to take her clothes off while they wrestled. He told her she could watch TV until eleven if she did, but she would have to keep it a secret. Lisa thought of all those late night programs she doesn't usually get to watch — then she thought about the request, got a 'funny feeling', as she put it, told him she didn't want to, and went to bed. The next morning she said to me: 'Mom, Uncle Pete asked me to do those funny things you told me about.' When I asked her what she meant, she said, 'Oh, you know — he wanted me to take my clothes off, but I didn't do it. Are you going to talk to him?' 'Yes, I am,' I told her, 'I'm sure glad you told me.' She gave me a hug and said: 'You know, Mom, I'm glad you told me no more secrets!'"*

Lisa was able to prevent a sexual assault. She was able to react before she was trapped by uncertainty, shame or confusion. She knew that her mother would want to hear about what happened, and would believe her. Lisa was not taken totally by surprise because her parents had provided her with information about sexual assault. Lisa had an advantage over many children. Not many parents have talked to their children about sexual assault and given them information about what might happen, and what steps they could take to protect themselves, for many different reasons:

1

"I don't want to confuse her with information she is too young to understand."

"I'm afraid that talking about sexual assault will cause my children to form warped ideas about sex — that it's brutal or scary."

"I don't know what I would say — I don't want to say the wrong thing."

Sexual assault is hard to talk about. It has long been a subject surrounded by secrecy and taboos. Although public awareness of the problem has increased dramatically in the past five years, it is still difficult to find helpful, practical information about children and sexual assault. It is even harder to find useful ideas about how to talk to children about sexual assault.

"Most of what I've heard is from the newspapers. I certainly don't want to scare my children with those horror stories."

Many parents feel a sense of helplessness about preventing the sexual assault of children.

"I don't know how to do it."

"If it's going to happen, it will. I wouldn't want to increase my child's guilt by pretending s/he could have stopped it."

"My only hope is that my child already has enough sense to be able to realize what is exploitation."

We wrote this book to change that. This book provides information and ideas to overcome the sense of helplessness and begin to stop the sexual victimization of children. We suggest some practical and positive actions to break the silence which has made children so vulnerable in the past. We want parents to talk to their kids about sexual assault. By ending the silence and mystery surrounding the subject, some children will be able to prevent a sexual assault, some will be able to keep one from progressing to a more serious level, and some will be able to get help from parents or other adults if they are victimized.

Most books about sexual assault are based on painful case histories. Not this book. We avoid harsh, unforgettable images. It's not necessary to know numerous case histories to be able to help protect your child.

Traditionally, children have been warned about strangers, in hopes that keeping kids away from strangers and weirdos will keep them safe. However, strangers account for only 10 or 15 percent of the offenders of children. The most common sexual assaults on children are by someone known to them who takes advantage of the child's trust. Telling kids only about strangers leaves them much more vulnerable than they need to be.

Parents also set limits on kids' behavior: not letting them walk home in the dark, play in the park alone, go to the bathroom at the movies alone, or take shortcuts home from school. Beyond that, kids get very little information. In fact, they are rarely even told *why* they are being warned about strangers.

> *"I really think that the chances of this happening to my daughter are so small that it's not worth it to frighten her by trying to talk to her about it."*

> *"I've got to admit that I never considered sexual assault as a real problem for my children. I've always thought that if you are careful, it wouldn't happen."*

What are the chances that a child will be sexually assaulted?

Chances are that we all know someone who has been a victim, even if we are not aware of it.

- In the United States, at least one in four females is assaulted before reaching the age of thirteen. (1)

Both boys and girls are victimized, though girls are more often than boys.

- Ten percent of victims reporting are boys. (2)

Young children, even preschoolers, are assaulted.

- At least ten percent of children who are assaulted are under five. (3)

The numbers vary from study to study, but all are overwhelmingly high.

- There are more children between eight and twelve reporting sexual assault than teenagers. (4) From 30 to 46 percent of all children are sexually assaulted in some way before the age of eighteen. (5)

(1) Alfred Kinsey, *et al., Sexual Behavior of the Human Female* (Philadelphia: W.B. Saunders, 1953).

(2) Sexual Assault Center, Harborview Medical Center, Seattle, WA, 1979.

(3) Children's Hospital National Medical Center, Washington, D.C.

(4) National Committee for Prevention of Child Abuse, "Basic Facts About Sexual Child Abuse."

(5) Child Sexual Abuse Prevention Project, Hennepin County Attorney's Office, Minneapolis, MN.

Are some children more vulnerable than others — or are all kids equally vulnerable? It is known that children are victimized regardless of their intelligence, race, age, neighborhood, social class or family income. As more is learned about sexual assault, more will be learned about factors which increase vulnerability, just as we are learning about the connections between stress and illness. Current information indicates that all children must be considered vulnerable to sexual assault — simply because they are children.

Kids are victimized in every community, every day, yet they're not getting much useful information about sexual assault.

"Our town had been bombarded by newspaper articles about a local rapist. Everyone was frightened. One of his victims lived in our neighborhood — she is a young girl. My neighbors were forming car pools to drive their kids to school. One morning my neighbor's daughter was out delivering newspapers before school when a police car pulled up. The officer told her there was a crazy rapist around loose, that he liked girls and that she had better be really careful. She was so frightened by this that she went home immediately and wouldn't leave the house. I think it is sad that a well-meaning police officer could frighten her so much. What she needed was some useful information. She needed to know how this crazy guy might make an approach and what she could do to protect herself. Scaring her to death didn't make her any safer."

Parents provide their children with many kinds of safety information: kids are buckled into seatbelts, taught to avoid poisonous plants, medicines and household chemicals, and warned about talking to strangers.

"I've practiced fire drills with my children since they were four. I know that fire is something that might be

frightening to them. It is to me, especially since we had a fire in our home years ago. But I don't know any better way to protect them. I think they actually feel safer knowing what to do in an emergency. When they hear the smoke alarm, they know they are to climb out their window without bothering to get dressed and wait for us on the sidewalk.''

We hope this book will help parents incorporate information about sexual assault into their general teachings about personal safety. Having some information about sexual assault can influence a child's response to the initial approach of an offender. Some assaults will be prevented, because a child who has some awareness of the problem is better able to protect her/himself. Others will be less serious, because the child is more likely to talk about it — more likely to ask for help before that first contact progresses into a more serious encounter.

There are many ways to help our children protect themselves. Many times, a traumatic incident can be stopped simply by a child saying "No!" in a loud voice.

"I teach a class for kids which includes information about sexual assault and some practicing of body awareness exercises. I had a girl in that class who met up with a stranger in a car on the way to school. He pulled up next to her and said in a very loud voice, 'Get in my car.' She said "No" and ran to school as fast as she could. She was so proud of herself she told the principal and her teacher, and together they called everybody — me, her parents, the police and Rape Relief.''

How to Use This Book

The words used in this book were chosen for particular reasons. We use the term "sexual assault" because other terms (sexual abuse, child molestation, sexual misuse) seem to minimize the seriousness and potential harm of a childhood sexual assault. We have also avoided the use of the word "fondling". Fondling has an implication of affection and tenderness — just the opposite of what is going on during an assault. We use the term "handling" instead. We use the pronoun "he" to describe offenders because most are men, although there are occasional female offenders. We use "s/he" in reference to children, because both male and female children are assaulted, although girls are victimized more often.

This book is a gathering of ideas and suggestions from many sources, but especially parents. We offer a variety of approaches to talking about sexual assault in the hopes that each family can find something of use. It's not necessary to read this book from cover to cover. Chapters are arranged so that parents with particular interests can locate the sections they need. For instance, if you are a parent picking up this book because your child has been sexually assaulted, you will want to turn to Chapters 8 and 9 first. Those chapters deal with helping a child who's been assaulted. The rest of the book focuses on prevention.

If you've wanted to bring up the subject with your child but just didn't know how to begin, Chapters 4, 5 and 6 will help. Maybe you're a parent who has been talking with your child about sexual assault already; you might be most interested in the games which can reinforce prevention ideas. They are together in Chapter 7. Tips on listening for children's messages about assault are found in Chapter 8. And, if you wish to be part of a community effort, Chapter 11 has some ideas. We've summarized our "Action Suggestions for Parents" on page 87. Finally, a list of Resources includes agencies, model programs, books and films.

We hope this book generates even more ideas and action!

Chapter 2

What Is the Sexual Assault of a Child?

Because the words sexual assault bring to mind a "dirty old man who jumps out from behind the bushes" or who "hangs around the school yard with dirty pictures until he can grab a kid," it is hard to imagine children preventing an assault. However, most sexual assaults don't happen that way.

What we fear	*What is more likely to happen*
A dangerous weird stranger	A person they know (85 percent of the time)
Violent attack	Bribery and threats rather than extreme physical force
Out of the blue, surprise	A situation that develops gradually over a period of time
Isolated extreme incident	Frequent incidents taking many forms

A Stranger vs. Someone Known to the Child

A child is much more likely to be sexually assaulted by someone s/he knows and trusts. One year, sexual assaults within the family (incest) accounted for almost half of the total number of children under 16 who used the services of the Sexual Assault Center in Seattle. Total strangers to the child accounted for 17 percent of the assaults that year, and 31 percent were acquaintances of the child (neighbors, babysitters).

"Word had spread all through my daughter's junior high that one of the students had been sexually assaulted. Many parents had warned their kids to be careful of the offender (who had not been arrested.). Those kids were so hyped they were afraid to leave the playground. Many were bunched together, afraid to walk home. But for all that fear of strangers on the streets,.this particular child had been assaulted by a friend of the family."

Violent Attacks vs. Bribery and Threats

Nobody expects kids to stand up to a violent attack. But most kids are not hurt physically during a sexual assault — most childhood sexual assaults don't involve that kind of force. Kids can learn to recognize the kinds of force that are more likely to be used against them.

Sometimes the force used is obvious. It may take the form of threats of harm or punishment to the child, withdrawal of affection, harm to the offender or threats to the family:

"I'll go to jail if you tell anyone."

"If you don't do this, you'll get into trouble."

"The family will break up if you tell."

"I won't like you anymore."

Other times bribery, or trading on the affection of the child may be used:

"I'll let you watch TV."

"Come see the kittens."

"What's the matter? Don't you like me?"

The offender may apply force (coercion) by saying:

"This is just our secret."

"They won't like you if they know you've done this."

Sometimes the force is more subtle, and difficult to recognize, such as involving the child in overcoming feelings that something is wrong:

"I'm doing this because I love you."

"It's OK — everybody does this."

An adult can take advantage of a position of trust and lead the child into a situation where s/he feels powerless to turn to other adults for help. The age difference of an adult or older child is assumed to represent force. There may be no appearance of force because the offender has relied on the child's ignorance, lack of a clear sense of being hurt or lack of a way to get help in the initial stages.

Children must rely on caring adults to protect them. For children to protect themselves from adults, they need the help of another adult.

"My little girl visits at her mother's house on a regular basis. She encounters there her mother's boyfriend, a big man, gruff and teasing. One day when I was dropping her off, he tripped her while trying to step on her shoe laces. She made a noise, didn't actually say anything, beat a retreat for her mother's door, and went into the room that is hers when she is there. When she got home I asked what had happened and whether or not she felt like she could do something herself. She said she wasn't sure because she wasn't sure he cared. She knew that what she said only made a difference if he cared about how she felt. Since she thought he didn't care, she decided to get help from her mother."

As parents we often forget the power adults have over children. Because we care about them, our children can seem very powerful to us. In schools and other institutions, or even at home, children may be taught to obey all adults and that any adult has the authority to tell a child what to do. We can help children minimize this vulnerability to adults.

Out of the Blue vs. Gradually Developing Situation

Most sexual assaults of children follow the pattern of a gradually escalating situation. It may, in the beginning, involve marginally inappropriate behavior, such as tickling a child beyond the point of a game, or touching a child on the buttocks or breast but acting as if it is accidental or happened in the course of play. This may be how the sexual assault begins and ends. The child may be aware only of a sense of discomfort. Sometimes, however, this continues until the contact is obviously sexual. This gradual escalation of contact leaves room for alert children to get help, if they have enough information to know that what they are experiencing is not all right.

Isolated Incident vs. Frequent Incidents in Many Forms

Sexual assault is any forced sexual contact. The forms of sexual contact can vary greatly. Contrary to the fear that small children will be forced to have sexual intercourse, the most common forms of sexual assault are handling and exhibitionism. The contact may involve handling of the child's genitals, or requests for handling by an older child or adult. Some assaults involve no physical contact. A child may be forced to look at the genitals of an older child or adult, or the child may be asked to undress or otherwise expose her/himself. Sometimes the contact is oral, sometimes it includes attempts at penetration of the vagina or anus, and sometimes, although rarely, actual penetration may occur.

Because some of these forms of contact (exposure, handling) are so common, some people feel that sexual assault or attempts are just part of growing up and if adults didn't make such a big deal out of them, they wouldn't be particularly traumatic to the child. However, studies of adults who were assaulted as children indicate that even those forms that involve no physical contact can be damaging and traumatic to the child — because it is done in an atmosphere of exploitation or violence. For most children, an assault can be traumatic in any one of a variety of ways. It can cause generalized fear and mistrust, it can create feelings of guilt and shame with destructive results to a child's self-image, it can cause depression, school disruption, family difficulties and more. But because the forms of contact are far less extreme than those feared, a child has opportunities to evade continued assaults if s/he knows what to do.

Because the person who approaches a child in order to gain sexual contact is usually known and trusted and the onset is usually gradual, there are chances to prevent an approach from turning into a sexual assault. Many potential sexual assaults can be prevented, not by superhuman children who respond heroically, but by children who have learned something about sexual assault and are not caught by surprise, trapped by shame or immobilized by confusion.

Chapter 3
How Can I Protect My Child?

Parents want to protect their children without having to talk to them about this awful thing and burdening them with the dreadful realities of the world. So we keep kids in sight, don't let them play in the woods, make sure they dress properly and don't do anything out of line and hope for the best. We teach them about strangers and get mad at them if they break a rule.

*"And now you say that isn't enough? Well, what is?
What can we do? Maybe we should just forget this
whole thing. Maybe it doesn't really hurt kids anyway,
if we would just get over being so uptight. And
anyway, I don't want to be suspicious of everybody."*

The information about who offenders are and how an assault
takes place leads to the conclusion that keeping children
close by and teaching them about strangers does not provide
much protection. But we don't want our children to be mis-
trustful of everybody. So, what can we do?

Unwanted Touch

We can monitor adults and older children around our children with the recognition that an assault, behavior leading to
an assault, or even harmless behavior (which nevertheless
may teach our children that they don't control who touches
them), may come from someone we have liked and trusted
— indeed, even someone we *still* like and trust. Many sexual
assaults take advantage of a child's dependency on adults
for protection. Children may feel that parents and other
adults are all-powerful, that they have eyes in the back of
their heads and that they always know what's going on.

*"When I was seven or eight, the man next door liked
me to sit on his lap when he and my parents were
having coffee. He liked to hug me. I liked him too, but
sometimes I felt awkward, and wanted to get away. I
remember looking around the room to see what my parents thought. I wondered why no one ever said anything. I didn't know what to do. It never occurred to me
that my parents didn't know what was going on."*

This recognition leads to some specific actions.

"My four year old son was being examined by the

pediatrician. I noticed the doctor was telling a story and looking around as though he were trying to distract my son. Suddenly the doctor sneaked his hand in my son's underpants to examine him. It was such a surprise. You should have seen the expression on my son's face. I stopped the exam right there. I held my son and asked him if it made him feel bad to be surprised like that. I suggested to the doctor that he explain what he was going to do next."

We can back up our children's right to say "no" and have it respected by noticing and acting on our children's discomfort.

"It seems many people tend to regard children as objects. When a child cries because a stranger is picking her/him up (the grocery clerk, a long lost relative) the child is labeled cranky, fussy or unfriendly. Such situations have caused me to become protective and ask the 'toucher' to please listen to my child."

"We were leaving after dinner with some old family friends. I noticed my youngest daughter was called over to Bob and he was whispering in her ear. I saw her take her shy, no-I-don't-want-to pose. He was pointing to his cheek saying, 'Come on, right here.' She shook her head 'No' again. I got up quietly and said, 'Come here, let's get ready to go.' I knew Bob meant no harm, but I didn't want my daughter to learn to kiss anyone she didn't want to, and I wanted her to know I would provide her some protection."

Actions like these can help children learn to take their feelings seriously and demonstrate that we as parents take their right to say "no" seriously.

Sometimes it doesn't seem possible to change a situation which ignores a child's feelings:

"I hate watching my three year old cry while she is thrown into the air, smooched on, and bounced from one relative to the next, before we are allowed to leave. My husband says that's how it has always been. What can I do?"

Talking to a child even this young about how s/he might like to change the situation may help to counter the idea that the child has to put up with all situations of being touched and not liking it. Comforting her/him about being passed around instead of passing it off can help the child feel that her/his feelings are important and won't just be ignored.

We can notice when children are being bullied or taken advantage of by friends of older brothers or sisters. Talking to both children about the friend to point out how the younger child is being tricked and bullied can help her/him figure out how to stop it. Or s/he may ask the brother or sister not to have the friend around, at least not without warning.

We can provide protection by demonstrating to our children that we will take seriously what they say about the way people treat them and help them figure out what to do.

"My children complained to me about the neighbor who lets them use his pool to swim. They said he swears and teases them. Once I would have told them to just never mind and not to let it bother them. This time I decided to talk about what they might want to do about it, since they didn't want to stop swimming. They said it was all right as long as I knew about it. They wanted to know if it was okay for him to be doing that, and they were relieved that I thought it wasn't."

This form of protection may be especially valuable when the person is an authority to the child in some way, such as a church youth leader, a coach, or an adult at school. Children need to know that we won't automatically assume the people in authority are right and they are wrong.

"Our daughter's soccer coach doubled their soccer practice time because 'some of the kids were lazy'. She didn't like that because it didn't seem fair to punish all the kids for what some of them do. We told her she didn't have to like it, she could tell him she didn't think it was fair, but she was going to have to make her own choice about doing the extra practice."

We can refuse to leave our children in the company of adults, relatives or friends of the family we do not trust, either because of something we have observed, something the child has said about the person, or just because of some feeling. Trusting a feeling or intuition about the potential of someone to sexually assault a child is difficult because sexual offenders do not have the appearance of being dangerous. They are often described as nice people, or being from a nice family. Adults may hold positions of authority in the community or have other positions which apparently contradict the possibility of sexual assault (a coach, teacher, or religious leader).

Further confusion arises from the current notion that sexual offenders are psychologically abnormal or crazy. Whatever the truth about offenders' craziness, they rarely appear "crazy."

"We were building on the house we had just moved into when Don, a neighborhood boy, started hanging around. He offered to help and seemed to enjoy the work. Sometime later, my wife and I were planning to go out and our regular babysitter canceled unexpectedly. Don said that he would take care of our three year old boy so we decided to go. The next morning our little boy came to me in the kitchen and said, 'How come Don wanted me to look at his pee pee?' I said that I didn't know and asked him what he did. He said that he told him he wouldn't do it. I had a talk with Don later. Even though I work with children, it didn't occur to me to consider Don a potential danger to my child."

Clues to Take a Second Look

Without knowing more about the background of the neighborhood boy, it is impossible to say whether or not there were any clues or signals which might have served to alert a parent to danger. But studies of sexual offenders suggest that certain characteristics might be important indicators of potential danger. These are signals which may occur during interactions between a child and adult:

● Disrespect of a child's requests or person shown through repeated tickling, patting or attempts for physical contact not wanted by the child may indicate someone who does not know how to behave reasonably with children and who won't listen to the child's efforts to set limits.

> *"I learned to stay away from him because I know he doesn't care what I say about stopping," said an eight year old.*

● Someone who relates to a child in a sexual manner, flirting or carrying on with comments about a child being a "real charmer" or "knock out" can be a hazard, if only because it is another burden to a child to figure out what it means and how to respond. It also may be an ideal opportunity to talk to a child about behavior which causes discomfort.

● While people with generous impulses may invite children into their homes, someone who consistently entices children to his house and into activities should be checked out somehow.

> *"He and his wife always had the children over for cookies and they watched TV there sometimes. I was stunned when my little girl told me he had approached her."*

- If a child indicates discomfort with someone or tries to avoid him, s/he is trying to give an important warning. Even if s/he does not have the words for what is troubling her/him and the problem may turn out to be minor, nothing can be assumed without talking carefully with the child.

  "My daughter suddenly became frightened of a friend of my husband. When I talked with her she just said, 'I don't know, he just looks different, I feel like I don't know him.' My husband and I finally remembered the friend had come back from vacation with a tan and a beard. We asked her to notice the next time he came whether or not that was why he looked different. It was."

There are also some personal characteristics which many sexual offenders share (although no single item is an *absolute* signal):

- A rigid and authoritarian background, such as military, religious, or a punitive family, is one of the characteristics.

- Heavy alcohol use is a danger sign. One-third of sexual assaults appear to involve the use of alcohol by offenders. Alcohol use is a rationalization used by many offenders for doing something they know they shouldn't. Young children around heavy alcohol users are at risk.

- Someone who was abused as a child seems more likely to abuse as an adult.

- Men who batter their wives will frequently abuse their children as well, sometimes sexually. They may also abuse other children.

*"I'm afraid the man my sister is married to is mean to
her. I want her to come visit me, but he always comes
too, and I worry about my children."*

● Social isolation is a characteristic sometimes listed in
connection with sexual offenders, both adult and adolescent. Someone with difficulty relating to people of the
same age, may choose children as companions and enjoy
the position of power the age advantage gives him.

● A previous sexual offense. Stories about lies and setups
are the most common form of denial by a sexual offender. It is easier to believe the stories than to believe that
someone we know is a sexual offender.

*"My sister's oldest just came back from California.
He got in some trouble with the authorities over a sexual offense. He says it was a setup and the family
believes him, but I'm worried about the other children
in the family."*

Even if the evidence wasn't sufficient for a conviction, it
doesn't mean the child wasn't telling the truth. Legal
proceedings are intended to safeguard constitutional
rights. That doesn't mean someone who has been
accused of a sexual offense is safe around children
without supervision.

Teenagers who commit sexual offenses sometimes come
from families which are abusive or very authoritarian, or
alcoholic. They lack friends their own age, may be picked on
by other kids, and choose younger children as companions.

This is not a complete list, and nothing on it is a certain
indicator of danger. Nor does every sexual offender have one
of these characteristics. Other characteristics, such as
discomfort with sexuality, are unlikely to appear in everyday
interactions. Anybody who has chronic difficulties in life, a

history of assaultive behavior, employment problems, or personal difficulties may be worth keeping an eye on. But there are others who won't give us any clue. Sometimes intuition says, "There is danger here," but sometimes it doesn't, because sexual assault is so different from what we may have believed it to be. These signs or characteristics can be added to the information we use to decide to take a second look at someone who is going to be in a position to take advantage of our children.

Babysitters

Parents can increase the amount of protection in a care-taking situation through a few deliberate steps:

- *We can* screen babysitters, with sexual assault as one of the considerations. The list of danger signals may provide some clues when there is a choice of sitters. Using only girls for sitters does not solve the problem and may even eliminate a good boy sitter. Screening babysitters means talking to them or to other parents enough to know how responsible they are and how well they understand their task.

> "I was appalled when I came home to find the house looking like a tornado had gone through. I asked the girls what had happened and they said 'Nothing'. Eventually the story came out. The babysitter had invited the neighborhood kids (ages six to sixteen) over for some fun and games. I don't think anything serious happened, although I certainly can't know for sure. I should have taken my suspicions about her seriously. I thought that something was not quite right about her preferring younger kids for company. Then I found out that she was allowed to smoke by one parent and the other parent didn't know. She didn't like to talk to adults, but I thought most teenagers don't.

*All together it should have been obvious, but I just
didn't trust my feelings enough."*

- *We can* do more than say, "Now mind the babysitter and
  do what s/he tells you." Preparing children for the babysitter can include talking about both the rules you expect
  them to obey (safety rules, house rules, meal and
  bedtime routines) and the possible sitter requests they
  should not obey, such as being asked to do something
  they don't understand, being threatened with trouble if
  they don't do something, or being offered a special treat
  for not telling about something.

  Chapters 4 and 5 contain many tools which can be used
  to prepare children to be left with a sitter. "What if"
  games work well also (see Chapter 7).

- *We can* also prepare carefully with the caretaker. Explain that our children don't keep secrets and will tell us
  if something goes wrong. We should say that our children have permission to say "no" if they don't understand a request. If we carefully review the family rules
  there will be less likelihood of a misunderstanding
  between the sitter and the children.

- Then *we can* follow-up with our children and sitter and
  find out how they each feel about their time together. If a
  child shows a sudden change of feeling for a previously
  liked babysitter, or protests being left with someone in
  particular, it may be time to take a look at the interactions between the sitter and child. If a pattern of
  talking about caretaking situations is established, the
  child may feel better able to speak up if a situation arises
  which needs attention.

No matter what we do, there are limits to the protection
we can give children. We may be genuinely handicapped in

keeping children away from someone we are suspicious of. A
friend of one's spouse, an ex-spouse, a step-parent in a
friend's home, any of these may be in contact with our
children because of the family relationship or because the
children would not be able to function under restrictions that
might be imposed to limit contact. Even without those extra
difficulties, children grow and begin spending time with
people we can't monitor. So we need to prepare children to
protect themselves from unwanted sexual contact. We can
talk to them, play prevention games with them, and be sure
that they know they can come to us with a problem.

Chapter 4
Where Do I Begin?

What Do They Already Know?

Talking to children about sexual assault begins with
finding out what they already know. Many children have
been given warnings about strangers or have seen reports of
kidnappings, rapes or murder on TV or in the newspaper.
We may find they have some notion of a hairy stranger
leaping out of the bushes at them, or a picture of someone
different from them, black if they are white, white if they are
black, approaching them on the way to school and taking
them far away from their parents forever. If we ask them
what the stranger is going to do, the answers may range
from, "hack me into a thousand pieces" to "make me take
my clothes off."

> "When I was five, my mother said, 'There, that's what
> rape is' when she and I saw some dogs mating. Until I
> grew up, I thought that rape was when you walked bent
> over because someone had jumped on you and broken
> your back."

Children who have been given information at school or at home may be confused about who a stranger is. One child decided that if someone offered her some candy and she wanted it, the person wasn't a stranger, but if she didn't want it, then he was. Another child reported after a talk at school that he didn't have to worry anymore because he could tell if someone was around who might do something weird. When asked how he could do that, he replied that they would have bandages on their heads because they are sick in the head.

> *"I know some children who were home alone and let a man come in who said he needed to use the telephone. Despite having been warned about letting strangers in, they said they trusted him because he was so clean, neat and rich-looking."*

We can find out what children already know by asking them questions.

> *"Who are you afraid of?"*

> *"What are they going to do?"*

> *"Why aren't you supposed to let people into the house?"*

If the child is older we can ask if s/he knows what rape is. Rape may be the only word children have heard. Although they may not know what it is, finding out what they think it is may tell us what they know about sexual assault.

Vocabulary

As we talk to our children to find out what they already know and what they believe, we can begin listening for words or phrases that mean something different to the child than to us.

*"I use the words 'get into trouble' to mean begin to be
in danger, but my children have only one meaning for
that phrase and it is to 'get into trouble' with an adult
or authority figure, and be punished or yelled at."*

Another word which may be used differently is the word
"hurt". Children usually understand the word to mean
physically painful. They may extend the meaning to
"hurting someone's feelings" but not much beyond. Adults
use the word in a much more general way. The more confusing words we find in the beginning, the more certain we
can be that our children will understand what we are saying
as we want them to.

Another set of words needed are those for the body parts.
Medical people would like us to use the specific anatomical
terms with our children so that when a child needs medical
care s/he can describe specifically what part of her/his body
is in need of care. Children as young as two or three can
learn and use the correct words. Using the correct terms can
help overcome the idea that there are parts of the body to be
ashamed of or which cannot be talked about. Using the
specific terms makes explaining what might happen if someone sexually assaulted someone else much easier. A
community crisis center in Oregon uses sexually
complete dolls to talk with children about body parts (see
"Resources"). If the explanation is made clear enough,
young children are less likely to develop more general
frightening ideas. Children can deal with a specific explanation with an "Oooh ick" or "That's gross" instead of vague
fears.

*"My younger daughter, nine, decided to go tell a couple
of neighbors about the sexual assault that happened to
her sister, and to make arrangements for coming home
from school with them. She told them that there was a
man out there 'threatening people with his penis.' The
mother's mouth dropped open and the kids started*

*giggling. But my daughter came home and wanted to
know why they were giggling. She didn't have any discomfort about what she said, and it certainly seemed
like an accurate description of what happened."*

Some people suggest the use of the term "private parts" as
an alternative when the use of the correct anatomical terms
is inconsistent with family values. To use the term, it is necessary that the children and adults agree on what parts of
the body are included in the idea of "private parts". One
way to describe private parts is to call it the area covered by
their bathing suit or their underwear.

Because children are scolded for using slang words for
body parts, they seem to have the idea they cannot talk
about their body. And children have some strange usages.
Many use the word "bottom" to refer to their body from the
waist to the top of the thighs. Many girls have no word which
they are comfortable using for their chest, or breasts.
Lacking the words to talk about parts of their body makes it
much harder for children to tell us if someone has tried to
touch them in those areas. Comfort with the words and with
their bodies can help children get help when they need it.
Developing this common understanding and vocabulary
can't be done all at once. It goes on as the child is ready for
more, and we see it is time for new information.

Many of us may be uncomfortable with the words or afraid
that we will give our children the idea that they can't talk
about this without upsetting us.

*"I've sat down with my son to talk about lots of things
we never talked about when I was growing up. Even
though I can't keep my stomach from tightening up and
I get a little sweaty, I try really hard not to pass along
the message that it's not okay to talk about certain
parts of his body."*

This discomfort about saying the right words and not

wanting to confuse the child can be lessened in several ways. One is to say, "I sure would like to be able to talk about this more easily, and I am practicing, but it is still hard for me." Children are less likely to be confused about what is being said to them when the tensions and discomfort are accurately labeled for them. Rehearsing alone in the car, in front of a mirror, or with a friend can increase our comfort too.

Confusing Sexual Assault and Sex

Clearing up misunderstandings and talking over words can get us started, but often there are other barriers. Many parents are concerned that talking about sexual assault will confuse children about sexuality and deprive them of a pleasurable adult experience. One of the ways to overcome this difficulty is to be sure that children have very complete and accurate information about sexuality and how it works as a positive force before talking about sexual assault in any way.

> "I have a friend who works for a rape crisis center. She appears on a poster which we saw at the medical clinic one day. My ten year old boy asked me what rape was and I didn't know what to say to him. I didn't want him to feel badly about being a boy and I didn't want him to think that sex was always bad, so I went and bought a sex education book for kids and talked to him about that before I tried to explain rape to him."

Sexual assault can be talked about as a separate subject with no mention of sexuality. It can be talked about as a violent and mean thing that some people do that happens to involve those parts of the body. The only problem with this approach is that, while an assault may be confusing or surprising, it may not seem mean or violent to the child immediately.

The confusion between sexual assault and sexuality can be handled by talking about how nice things can be unpleasant or mean if they aren't wanted. We can remind children of times when someone has tickled them past the point of fun, or times when they have been wrestling with someone who wouldn't quit. Or we can talk about other forms of touch like a hug that are nice when they are wanted but feel bad when they aren't.

> *"But how can you talk to kids without scaring them about everybody if you tell them that someone they know and like might assault them?"*

Children trust or mistrust people for reasons that may have nothing to do with how trustworthy that person is. They may be afraid of someone because he looks different and trust someone because he gives them treats. Children can learn other clues without becoming more fearful. Children who know exactly what to be watching for and know that they can tell someone and get help are going to be less fearful, not more.

Where to Start

Once we have decided how to take care of our concerns, we still have to actually find a time and talk to our children. We have prepared our children by finding out what they already know and decided on words we can all use and mean the same thing. Children don't usually ask questions unless an incident comes up, or an opportunity is created. Sometimes we decide to talk to our children immediately because we realize that someone around the children may be a danger to them. Sometimes after a divorce, one parent is concerned about people the other parent exposes the children to. Sometimes we would like to help our children protect themselves from a person in authority, a playground supervisor, a church leader or even a teacher. When this is the case, all we can do is start. "I am worried that someone may try to take advantage of you." Depending on the relationship to the child, the person may or may not be named.

"I was concerned about my three and a half year old son because a teenage boy was staying with us a while, and we didn't know him all that well. I told my son, 'Don't let anyone touch your penis, and I want to know about it if it happens.' I think it backfired. My son went around for days asking everybody, 'Can I see your penis?' including the teenager with us, who was quite surprised. I was embarrassed, but my husband said, 'It will pass,' and I think he is safer for having heard all that."

When the situation is less urgent than this, we can combine teachings about sexual assault with other safety teachings and gradually increase both the amount of information we give and the amount of independence of our children. When we first start teaching about cars and streets, we tell children to stay away from the street, period. As they get older, they are allowed to cross quiet streets and begin making judgments about cars. Certainly, to start by defining rape to a two year old is not useful. But even toddlers do understand some of the suggestions in the following chapters.

Discussions can begin as soon as the child will understand. Many parents start talking specifically about sexual assault by the time a child is five.

"I started talking about all kinds of safety information to my daughter when she was four, the summer she started riding a Big Wheel tricycle. She rode on the sidewalk and I was in the house. I realized that she was out dealing with the neighborhood on her own."

In the same way, we can begin talking about sexual assault in the easiest terms: "Sometimes people will do things that don't seem right, and I want you to tell me if that happens." Then go on to the material which is harder to understand and explain.

In either case, the timing will be easier if we don't limit ourselves to talking only in quiet, private places.

> *"Some of the best conversations I've had have been at the dinner table, because the atmosphere is open and light."*

The car can be a good place to talk. Seeing hitchhikers will sometimes start conversations. If nothing spontaneously triggers talking, just starting in seems more acceptable in cars. Sometimes leaving a book or newspaper article around will work to start conversations with older children. Sometimes children will begin asking questions if they learn that something has happened to a friend of theirs. Even though the child asks a question, it is important not to jump in with all the information at once without finding out for sure what the child is asking. After each discussion with a child, follow up a few days later with a question about whether s/he has more questions to ask. This can help everybody keep talking and help children believe that parents really are willing to talk about sexual assault.

Chapter 5
What Do I Say?

> *"When I first started thinking about sexual assault and wanting to talk to my daughters, I panicked at the thought of trying to get my newly formed ideas into words they could understand. Too much of what ran through my head were still my own questions."*

Exactly what we say to our children depends on our children's ages, our own values, languages, and our family structure. The goal is the same: to give our children enough specific information to recognize behavior which may be leading to a sexual assault or may be an assault.

*"If you live in rattlesnake country, you don't worry
about scaring your kids. You just tell them as much as
you can about what a rattlesnake looks like and sounds
like, and where they might run into one."*

In the past, warnings have been so vague that children
had no way to recognize that what was happening to them
was what the warnings were about.

To recognize an assault, children need to know what form
the contact may take, who might do it, and what kind of force
he may use.

Explaining Sexual Assault

*"Sexual assault is someone touching you, or making
you touch them when you are confused, or tricked
about the touching."*

Defining sexual assault in terms of touching is a
comfortable starting place. Adding the information that the
touch may be sexual is the next step.

*"It's any adult or older child touching your genitals,
anus, or breasts, or asking you to touch or look at the
adult's genitals."*

It's easier for children if they are comfortable with the use
of these words for body parts before you use them.

*"Someone may try to touch your crotch when you don't
want them to or someone may try to make you touch his
penis when you don't want to."*

None of these explanations is perfect. The search for a
definition that will work is an individual process. But the
more specific the definition, the less frightening and confusing the situation will be for the child, especially compared
to what they imagine.

"I find it most useful to develop a definition for myself to work from and then break it into pieces as I talk to the girls. The definition I use is the specific anatomical one. I don't use the words 'sexual assault', but incorporate my value judgments: 'It's no fair for someone to ask you to undress for them when you don't know why', or, 'Somebody might touch your breasts and pretend it's accidental.'"

Other examples:
Someone might . . . try to put his hands down your shirt or pants . . . ask you to lie down on a bed with him . . . keep rubbing up against you . . . undress in front of you for no good reason . . . ask to take pictures of you without any clothes on . . . try to kiss you on the mouth.

Who?

A child's response to the definition of sexual assault is often, "Ooh ick, who would try to do THAT? I would never let anybody close enough to me to do that!" Children think anyone who would do something that sounds so dreadful, would have to be a stranger. So in explaining "who", we are going to have to start with, "But it may not be a stranger. It would probably be someone you know."

"Like who?"

If there is someone in the environment about whom we are concerned, we may be able to say, "Like Mr. Q."

"But he's really nice."

And then we have the perfect opening for, "Even nice people do mean things sometimes. They may not even realize how mean they are."

"Well, he wouldn't do something like that."

We can still extend the opening.

> *"Okay, but if he ever does something you don't under-*
> *stand — either him touching you or him asking you to*
> *touch him — please come and talk to me about it,*
> *okay?"*

Frequently we cannot name a person. Either we have not
identified a person in the environment or the person can't be
named because of the child's loyalty (as in step-family or
family situations). But we can still provide the idea that we
want to know about anybody who touches in a way that
makes a child uncomfortable.

> *"I think the most important thing we can teach our kids*
> *is to trust their feelings of discomfort, NO MATTER*
> *WHO the person is."*

We can explain that everybody, adults included, makes mis-
takes and has problems. We can remind children about
people who don't know how to talk to them or how to touch
them in a way that feels okay. Usually the problems don't
show. But sometimes the problem people have is that they
try to have sexual contact with children. It is not up to the
child to try to help the person with the problem or even to
figure it out. All children need to do is to tell another adult
if anybody — friend of the family, older kid in the neighborhood, babysitter — does something they don't understand or
which makes them uncomfortable.

Force

Sometimes children can understand the "who" better
when we explain the kind of force someone might use. If
children understand that the other person doesn't usually
"hurt" them physically, but that what they do causes
"hurt" anyway, they may be able to understand that some-

one they might like could do such a thing.

We can talk about how sometimes "nice" people will try to bribe children into doing something they don't want to do. Children receive free things all the time, from lollipops at the bank to free nails at the hardware store. And often it is not clear what is expected in return. At the bank nothing is expected, at the hardware store maybe a big smile and a thank you. We can help children begin to make sense out of all this by talking about gifts, bribes and obligations.

"Gifts people give you just because they want you to have them, either because they enjoy giving, like Christmas presents, or because they want you to come back, like lollipops at the bank."

Bribes are given to get a person to do something they are not supposed to do, or might not want to do.

"I'll let you watch TV if you will lie for me."

"I'll let you feed the rabbits if you undress for me."

"I'll give you some of the candy I steal if you don't tell."

Bribes usually must be kept secret. When children are older, we may want to begin to explain obligations.

"Some people seem to expect something in return for a gift. If you aren't sure what it is they expect, maybe it would be better not to take the gift."

"Trades between two people of the same age, when each is willing to give up what he or she has to gain what the other one has, are fair. There isn't a trick or a bribe or bullying if it is a fair trade."

"Sometimes older children or adults will use tricks or threats to gain sexual contact, and that isn't a fair trade. If a trade must be kept secret, it is not okay."

Another form of force used against a child is trapping the child into breaking a rule and then threatening the child with punishment if s/he tells anybody about what is going on. Sometimes there isn't a spoken threat, but the child knows somehow that what is going on is wrong or will be upsetting to her/his parents and so doesn't say anything. And sometimes the other person says, "Don't tell anybody about this or you will get into trouble," or sometimes it is, "or I'll get into trouble."

Secrets

Secrets are a powerful force used against children. They range from the exclusive, "Let's keep this our little secret" to the threatening, "If you don't keep this secret, everybody will think you are awful." Some families therefore have a rule that there will be no secrets kept except between children of the same ages. Secrets are things which are always to be secret, and are different from surprises which are nice things we eventually want to share. Presents for another person are surprises, not secrets. It's fun to have surprises and it can be fun for children to have secrets between themselves, but it's not fair for an adult or an older child to ask a younger child to keep a secret, especially from her/his parents.

For example a babysitter might let the children do something in return for not telling the parents. The deal itself may be relatively harmless:

"We limit TV programs to those ok'd ahead of time. And we have told babysitters this. That makes more work for them I suppose and we discovered that one was letting the kids watch TV but making them promise

*not to tell or she would 'get them' on the school bus.
We used the opportunity to talk with the girls about
secrets and thanked them for telling us. We probably
won't use that babysitter again. "*

But deals like this have the effect of teaching children to
keep secrets in return for getting something they want. This
can be turned against them in a much more destructive way.
The secret itself is destructive because it is a wedge between
parents and children. Children often will act badly in order
to get an adult to realize there is a secret being kept.

With specific descriptions like these, children are in a
better position to avoid being tricked or exploited.

But What to Do?

One way to prepare a child to resist is to give some simple
examples of what might happen and some responses:

- If someone wants a hug and you don't want to do it, you
can say, "No thank you."

- If someone pats you on the bottom, you can tell her not
to.

- If someone wants you to sit on his lap, you can say, "Not
right now."

- If someone older wants to touch your penis you can run
away from him.

- If someone you know puts his hand on your shoulder and
it feels bad, you can remove it.

- If a relative always wants to give a sloppy kiss, you can
shake hands instead.

- If someone grabs you through your clothes, you can say, "Stop, that's not okay."

Here are more examples of situations and suggestions about what children can do.

- "What if you were at the movies, and some man grabbed your crotch? That happened to me once, and I didn't know what to do or who to tell. What you should do is say, 'Hey! Don't do that to me!' and move away from him and go tell the theatre manager what happened. The manager or you can call the police."

- "You play a lot at other people's houses and I'm not there with you. Something funny could happen, something that you are not sure is okay. What if you were near the bathroom and someone asked you to bring him some soap because he discovered he ran out after he was already in the tub. You could say, 'I'm not allowed to be in the bathroom with anyone else.' I want to know about any funny things like that."

- "If, for instance, after we went out and left you at home with the babysitter and she wanted to play with your penis, you should say, 'No, and I will tell my parents.'"

- "The babysitter might ask you to be naked for a while, and let her/him play or look at your vulva (penis). Say, 'No, that's not OK.' If 'no' doesn't work, then go next door to the Smith's, and tell them (or call me at work, or go to bed and lock your door).

- "If you were picking flowers at a neighbor's yard where you knew you shouldn't be picking flowers, and a man came out and said he wouldn't get mad if you would come inside and play a secret game, don't! He's trying to get you to do something you don't want to do by tricking you. Just because you made a mistake about picking the flowers doesn't mean you have to do what he says. Come home and tell me about the problem.''

We can help children rehearse phrases they could actually use. Children need to understand that they don't have to decide *why* the other person is doing what s/he is doing. If the child is uncomfortable with the touch or the request, s/he can say ''no'' in one of these ways or others.

Saying No

Saying ''no'' for a child may be very difficult in this situation. We can give some backup for younger children by suggesting they use family rules.

''Don't do that, it's against the rules in this house.''

''No, I can't do that. My mom told me not to.''

''I'm going to tell my father.''

With older children we can develop the idea that they have the right to be angry if someone tries anything like this. Anger is a powerful emotion which can be used to protect the child and to help her/him feel less victimized.

''When my daughter came in after a stranger tried to attack her, she was doubled over and holding her stomach. I asked her if she was going to be sick (throw up). She said, ''Mom, I was so angry, so angry.' I think that's why she got away.''

Teaching children how and when to say ''no'' can provide a useful protection. If we teach children when it is all right for them to say ''no'', it is more likely they will be able to stick to it when it is important. We teach children they can't say "No" when the request is to come to dinner or to otherwise obey a family rule. We can teach children to say, "I don't understand" or even, "How come?" when they don't understand the reason for a request. Children can be taught to save "No" for times when they really are going to stick to it. It will help children to say "No" to an approach if they have had this practice. We can allow children to say "No" or "No thank you" to unwanted treats or touch within the family, without explanation and without saying, "I'm sorry." Sometimes parents will want to know how a child is feeling and will want more information. We can be sure a child knows we respect her/his "No" if we say, "I accept your 'No'. Are you willing to talk about it, or tell me why you don't want that?" Children can also be taught to ignore taunts or teases about any "No's" to other children and to simply repeat them firmly. The "No" game in Chapter 7 is good practice.

The Right to Control Touch

If children are going to say "No" to an adult, they need to believe that they have the right to control who touches them and that they can get help enforcing that right from other adults. They need to know that we (or someone) will listen to them if they need to ask questions about behavior which makes them uncomfortable, without blaming them, or getting upset with them.

Children start out with the idea that they have some say over who touches them and how. They cry, fuss, scream, and otherwise indicate discomfort if they don't like how they are being handled or don't trust the person doing it.

"We were at the lodge for New Year's dinner with our daughter and friends. Everyone was sitting down as the waiter came up with the high chair. My daughter was standing there inspecting it when the waiter in a rush grabbed her, plopped her in the chair, snapped

*her in and rushed off. My daughter never could get
comfortable in the chair, and we didn't get to enjoy our
dinner.''*

They laugh, giggle, smile and coo when they like what is
going on. As children get older they are trying to make
choices about cuddling and not cuddling and getting close to
people. Unfortunately adults frequently ignore these efforts
to establish boundaries. We pat them on the head, catch
them by the arm, hug them and tickle them without checking
to see if the child wants the contact. If children learn to
ignore their feelings because they don't seem to matter, they
lose a valuable tool to protect themselves. If they can keep
and even talk about those feelings, they have a tool for
protecting themselves.

*"My eleven year old was talking to me about two of her
teachers. One of them really made her uncomfortable
even though he never really touched or did anything
she could name. She said it always felt like he was looking down her blouse. She really likes another teacher
who touches a lot and she isn't uncomfortable with
him.''*

We can help children learn not to ignore those feelings by
respecting them ourselves. If they pull away, tighten up or
make a face of some kind in response to touch we can say
something showing we recognize the action and are willing
to respect it.

Getting Help — It's Not Their Fault

If children recognize that an adult makes them uncomfortable, they need to be able to talk to another adult to get some
help or protection before they are trapped by some sense of
guilt or shame. What works against us is that children don't
like to tell us things that are going to upset us, make us mad,
or get them in trouble.

"My husband and I have worked and worked to try to get the girls to come to us if there is a problem of any kind. Our menagerie at home is one of the ways it comes up. Over and over again, we've had to discover that animals were missing or hurt; neither girl would say anything because they were afraid of getting in trouble. After we found a baby corn snake under the rug, and a goat in the wrong part of the barn (that they knew about but hadn't told us), we began to fear that the only way they would learn was if something terrible happened to one of the animals. So we talked with them about letting us know. The other day, they came to me right away after they had left the lid up on the snake's cage and she had gotten out. We found her immediately, not far away. I'm hoping that the idea that there is less harm done if an adult knows right away is going to be real now."

Children seem to spend a lot of time deciding whose fault some mishap is. And their ability to be honest about something they think is going to get them into trouble develops with age and isn't always very reliable. As parents we want to reward the efforts toward honesty without making it a way out of consequences which can't always be avoided.

"When our eight year old started getting the idea about being honest, she started coming to us saying, 'Yeah, I'm the one that trashed the playroom and didn't pick it up; aren't you glad I told you the truth?'"

Talking about a rule and its purpose can give a child an opportunity for taking responsibility for a choice and gives us an opportunity to talk about how breaking rules decreases the amount of help and protection we are able to give. Children seem to consistently break safety rules. Sometimes they get hurt, sometimes they don't. If they get hurt, restraining the "I told you so" is tough. We can tell our children that the purpose of the rule was to protect them, but if it didn't work, we still want to help. But in order to help we must know if a child is hurt either through breaking a rule or through being taken advantage of.

Children who face terrible punishment for misdeeds may be vulnerable to blackmail by older siblings or children in the neighborhood. "Oh, come with us, they will never know," is all too often followed by, "Do what we tell you or we'll tell your parents what you did today."

We can minimize the seriousness of an assault, or prevent a continuing assault, if children understand that they are not to blame if someone tricks, traps, or bribes them into sexual contact. To convince them of this we can say in as many ways as possible that if someone touches them in a sexual way and they didn't stop it for whatever reason, it is not their fault, and we want to help even if a rule has been broken.

Getting Help — Asking About Puzzling Adult Behavior

We can show a willingness to listen and answer questions by not telling a child how s/he feels or should feel. When the child acts shy around someone it is the difference between, "Oh, come on now, you know Uncle Jeff, don't be shy" and, "Oh, you don't remember Uncle Jeff," or, "Oh, you're not feeling sociable today, okay." Children ask embarrassing and poorly timed questions about personal characteristics of another person. We can *answer* questions like, "How come Aunt Josephine is so fat?" with, "I don't know," or, "Everybody is different and special in their own way," instead of, "Don't be rude!" If we allow such questions, then "How come Grandpa always puts me on his lap when I don't want to sit there" can be asked. If our children can ask us questions like these, it may help them ask early enough to stop an assault.

Responding to questions with full explanations instead of "Don't worry about it" will also encourage children to express concerns. Help them develop a plan or explanation of what they can do in response to their worry.

Older children may get help more quickly if they have the choice to talk to someone other than their parents. Children often have very mixed feelings about the person who assaulted them. They may need someone outside the family to talk to first. We can talk to children about who else they might talk to: a relative, family friend, mental health center, rape crisis center, or police are all possible places to get help.

This is the framework for helping children protect themselves. They need to know:

- what an assault is so that they can recognize behavior leading up to one;

- that they have the right to control who touches them and how;

- that they can ask us about puzzling adult behavior;

- that it's not their fault if something happens.

But this won't be convincing all at once, or in the same way to all children. As children grow, they will understand and be convinced about different information.

"I have never tried to tell my kids all of this at one time. One time the definition of rape comes up because of a newspaper headline, another time I will bring up how it is not their fault if an older child takes advantage of them. When I do it this way, I am not as worried about them misunderstanding what I am saying, and I can better relate what I want them to know to what is going on in their lives."

Chapter 6

When Is There Time to Talk?

Opportunities to talk about sexual assault arise frequently when we are alert to circumstances which might affect a child's response to a potential assault situation.

> *"When I first started wanting to talk to my little boy about sexual assault, I kept seeing opportunities vanish while I was trying to figure out what to say. After some practice and lots of lost opportunities, I see that there are lots of chances to talk about sexual assault without explaining the whole thing at once."*

Touching

Families differ greatly on how much touch and contact goes on between family members and on how touch is viewed. Children understand touch and their own feelings about it better if they have a chance to talk about different kinds of touch. The more experience children have talking about touch, the more likely they are to be able to stop touch that is exploitative, or at least to be able to talk about it and get help when it is needed.

> *"We are a very touching family. I would hate my child to have to size up every person who touches her. I think it's possible to be paranoid about all of this and instill doubt and fear in our kids."*

An explanation of touch which has been used in a pilot project in schools (see "Child Sexual Abuse Prevention Project, Minneapolis, MN" in "Resources") presents a continuum from "good touch" to "confusing touch" to "bad touch." Good touch makes people feel as if something has been given. If children are asked what kinds of touch feel good to them, they say petting an animal, playing games, cuddling. Bad touch hurts or makes people feel bad. Examples of bad touch are hitting, pushing and sexual assault. Children may include being spanked or even something we haven't thought of as unpleasant to them.

Between the two kinds of touch is confusing touch. Confusing touch just doesn't feel right. Maybe it is different from the way we touch in our family, or maybe it is touch which we don't like but tolerate to "be nice" to someone.

"My daughter came home sometime in the sixth grade talking about a boy who hit her, and I told her that he probably liked her and wanted her to pay attention to him. My daughter said that was real stupid, and she certainly wasn't going to pay attention to someone who had to hit her to get it. I felt foolish for responding with the age old thing I had been told. Hitting is a stupid way to get attention, and I'm glad my daughter recognized that."

Some activities like wrestling and tickling can be identified as touch which may start out as good, or as confusing, but then turn to bad touch.

"I remember tickling sessions with my mother and two brothers that moved from fun into what seemed like torture. Nobody in my family meant any harm, I'm sure, but my memories are vivid of that terrible feeling of saying 'Stop' and having everyone ignore it, and feeling as though I would be tickled to death."

Sometimes one person acts as if it were a game, and therefore good touch. The child doesn't have a chance and knows it, but doesn't have any way to call it what it is.

"I remember being held by the wrists by a friend of my

*father's. He wouldn't let go. I was struggling to get
away and he was making it like a wrestling match. I
bawled in the bathroom later — I really felt powerless
and bullied.''*

Experimental programs with children talking about touch
have demonstrated that when they have a chance to talk
about touch, they feel more comfortable giving and receiving
good touch and more capable of stopping bad touch. Discussions which are balanced between good touch and bad
touch will help overcome any negative influences of naming
bad touch. This can be a family exercise, talking about touch
in the family, how it seems to be given and received and
what is confusing about it.

Privacy and Boundaries

We can extend the discussion of good, bad, and confusing
touch into the area of privacy and boundaries. One of the
developmental chores of children is to develop boundaries
which are consistent with their family's beliefs about touch,
physical affection, privacy, and nudity. They will have an
easier time if we talk about some of those issues instead of
leaving them to guess.

We can help children develop those boundaries, recognize
when they have been crossed, and decide what to do. Where
we set boundaries is going to differ from family to family.
For families where the boundaries are very strict, the
message may be simple: "Nobody, not even you, should
touch your private parts." Children will be better protected
if this prohibition includes the idea that children are not to
blame if someone tricks, traps, or bribes them into sexual
contact. If children have been given the idea that only "bad"
children are touched or touch others sexually, they are more
likely to decide they are "bad" if someone takes advantage
of them. They will be more vulnerable to the idea that the
sexual assault is their fault, and that they will get in trouble

if they tell anyone.

In other families where the boundaries are not so strict, it is more complicated. With very young children, very simple situations and examples work best.

> *"I bathe with my three year old. I tell her to wash her own vulva and I will wash mine. She always wants to wash mine. When she asks why she can't, I answer that mine is mine, and she has her own to take care of. I am trying to get her to understand that she can take care of her own body. One of these times I'm going to add that, 'If anybody else wants to do that for you, I want to know'."*

As children reach six or seven they develop a growing sense of body privacy. They grow more private about who sees them in various stages of undress and begin to ask for privacy for bathing and changing clothes.

Children also develop the need for some private space which can be their own for some period of time. Children with their own rooms begin to ask others to knock, those without a room of their own create private space by monopolizing the bathroom for a time or finding a space outdoors where they can be alone. When children begin to express these needs, we can also introduce the idea that they have a space around them which should be respected even when other people are around. It can be called body space or safety bubble or whatever is appealing. We can reinforce the idea that no one has any more right to enter that space without permission than someone has the right to come into their room or other private space without permission.

For parents who do not want to take a chance on a child confusing sexual assault and sex, privacy can serve as an alternative way of explaining sexual assault.

> *"On the topic of rape, we explained to our daughter about the violation of her body by another without her*

*permission. We have used the following example. 'If a
door is closed, like your bedroom door, then another
person should not enter it without your permission.'
This example worked well in talking to her about what
constitutes rape.''*

With an older child, privacy can be related to sexual assault
by saying that it's not okay for anyone to invade personal
body space by touching sexual parts of the body.

*''I don't know what to think about my daughter. She is
eight, real friendly and cuddly. I don't want to dis-
courage her friendliness, but I worry that someone is
going to take it wrong.''*

A parent who has a worry like this needs to talk to the child.
There is no evidence that links nudity, flirting or extra
friendliness to sexual assault, but that doesn't mean that we
should ignore our feelings of vulnerability. The children may
not be in extra danger, but they may need more information
about nudity, touching, and affection.
    Sometimes children who are overly friendly may be
trading on physical affection to get what they want. Some
families inadvertently teach that approach: ''Give me a big
kiss and I'll give you a cookie.'' Sometimes the outside world
encourages it. Especially attractive children may easily learn
that the world is filled with more treats and fewer obstacles
if they give a hug instead of asking for what they want
directly. Parents can talk to children about how that feels
and what the limits of the trade can be. ''A smile for a nail,
but not more.'' Parents can be sure their own interactions
with the child do not encourage that kind of trade. The
affection a child offers may be taken as freely given,
negotiating separately for whatever the child wants.
    Nudity is another issue which fits in this confusing
picture. Young children are allowed a great deal of freedom
to move about without clothes. As children get older, some

seem to adopt modesty early and without any questions. Others persist past their parents' point of comfort with nude behavior, some of which may seem sexual, or sensuous. Children who are "too old to be running around that way" may need more information about what being nude means (it is certainly a confusing value in our society), or perhaps are testing some limits, or may simply enjoy the sensations of nudity. Find out what the child needs and reinforce the idea that no one has the right to take advantage of her/him no matter what the state of dress or undress.

"Playing doctor" is a game which ranges from simple curiosity to rehearsal for medical procedures to overt sensuality in meaning. Talking with children about playing doctor can provide an opportunity to be explicit about what is all right for someone else to do and what isn't all right. Maybe rehearsal for medical procedures is all right but no more.

Children who are allowed to play doctor with sexual overtones should know that if someone older tries to join them, they should stop the game and tell an adult. They should also understand that it is not fair to try to involve a younger child, because the younger child might misunderstand, be confused or scared. That is not all right.

There is much confusion about physical touch, affection, sensuality and sexuality in our culture. Nudity, friendliness and flirting are all part of that confusion. Anything we can do to help children clear up their own confusion and identify sexual touch coming from an older child or an adult as bad touch — and not their fault — will help them avoid a sexual assault.

School Happenings

A sexual assault may be linked to the school somehow. A letter might come home warning of an exposer who hangs around the school. Talking about it might start something like this:

"An exposer is a man who shows his penis. He might be in a car, or on the sidewalk. He is trying to scare someone. What you need to do is to get away from him, and tell someone about him quickly — me or someone at school. The police will want to know too. They'll want you to try to remember as much as you can (what he looked like, where he was)."

Children with specific information like this have been able to react just this way to an indecent exposer and may feel less victimized because they knew just what to do.

"My daughter's Bluebird group included a speaker from rape relief in her Camp Fire 'survival skills' program after school. There had been an exposer around her elementary school and lots of people were concerned. The speaker talked to them about what to do if it happened to them. About a week later, my daughter and her friend were walking home and there appeared a man exposing himself. They knew just what to do. They ran to the nearest house with a 'helping hand' in the window and from there called the police. They felt so proud of themselves."

Sometimes at school harassment takes a sexual form. Bra snapping, "pantsing," forced kissing, or other contact between children the same age may not seem that important to adults. But for children experiencing it, it can be torture, and counter to all those things we are trying to teach. Talking seriously with our children about these forms of harassment may even lead us to decide some form of intervention at school is needed. At the least we can take our children's concerns seriously and help them work out a plan they can use to escape the unpleasantness.

"When my daughter was in the sixth grade, a group of boys started the teasing and harassing that sometimes goes on at that age. The boys were snapping bras. The girls didn't know what to do about it, or how to stop it. We decided to meet with the class and talked to the kids about how unfair that sort of teasing was. We discovered that the boys had really been misinterpreting the girls' giggles and laughter. They thought that the girls thought it was funny and didn't realize the giggles were from embarrassment and not knowing what to do. When they realized the girls really didn't like it, they stopped."

Children may get into trouble in school settings when they question rules or adult requests. Children need to know they don't have to do everything an adult asks them to do. We can teach them to question requests if they don't understand. Unfortunately, that may not always be possible for children. Sometimes school people issue orders, commands or rules which children do not understand or which seem unfair. We can talk with children about how the unfairness feels, help them decide if they want to take any action, see if there is any assistance we can lend to the situation and repeat that we don't think that adults are always right. Then we can add that even school people do not have the authority to tell them to undress (except in P.E.) or to ask them to do anything which may seem sexual. We can offer to listen when the child feels something is unfair and not try to explain away the unfairness of an action. We can remind children that if a request:

● feels funny

● seems like it would separate her/him from other children

● goes against family rules

- involves a secret

- seems like an unearned special favor

they can refuse the request and expect our support in backing them.

Bullying

Children are often bullied at school and going to and from school. All children respond to bullying, some more successfully than others. Successful children can be encouraged to continue to develop those skills (as long as they are not violent or destructive). Children who lose to bullies can be encouraged to develop new reactions. They can ignore, bluff back, give the impression of being untouchable, or leave the situation. A child who can successfully manage an encounter with a bully has a much better chance of escaping an assault.

Children who are being intimidated by bigger kids may need help in discovering resources of their own to use against the bullies. Sometimes, bullies don't do anything if their bluff is called. Sometimes younger children can outrun or outsmart a bully if they are not trapped by feelings of powerlessness. If physical threats from other children are a consistent part of a child's environment, the child might benefit from a self-defense sport designed for children. The change in self-confidence developed through such training is often enough to end the situation.

Vulnerability

As we watch our children grow and play, we learn their special fondnesses and vulnerabilities.

"When I think about how my oldest child might be led to break the rules about not going with someone even if

s/he knows him, I think about someone offering a horseback ride, or saying that he had some baby animals for her to see, or that one of our animals was hurt. She was ready to walk out of the house one night late, because the neighbors had called to say our cat was up at their house.''

''I worry about my child believing someone who says, 'Your mommy just talked to me and she said for you to go with me.'''

If a child is helped to develop some specific ideas about how to respond to the questions or leads which s/he might be most likely to follow, s/he may be less vulnerable. Maybe one child would go for the use of a rock polisher, or a ride on a motorcycle, another might want to see unusual flowers or trees. These special interests and caring are what make people unique so we don't want to reduce the enthusiasm, we just want to help children find ways to lessen their own special vulnerability.

Modeling

Another powerful tool we have to help our children learn how to say ''No'' and refuse requests they don't understand is to show them. When, as adults, we refuse a request or move away from those who get too close, we can point out to our children what we did and why.

Turning away door-to-door salespeople, ending unwanted telephone sales calls, and saying ''No'' to a request from a friend are all opportunities for adults to demonstrate possible responses for children.

Another way we can ''show'' our children is through games.

Chapter 7
Can Games Help Teach Prevention?

Children learn about the world through play. Parents can put games to use to build on the ideas introduced through talking.

One way to start is to be sure that children aren't learning to be powerless through tickling or wrestling sessions they can't stop when the activity is no longer fun. Set up rules with them about only hollering "No" or "Stop" when they are really ready to stop. The mock protest part of the fun can be screams and giggles or even standard phrases like "Don't do that" or "Not again, not again!" But "No!" and "Stop!" can be the signal words that the activity should end. Then be sure to stick to that rule and be sure that other adults and older children respect the "No!" or "Stop!" too.

Games and organized sports may also be useful to counter the learned physical helplessness which can work against children protecting themselves. Many girls, for example, learn by the age of three or four that little girls are "supposed" to sit and play quietly, not run around and play rough and tumble. As girls get older, they may also be challenged to a "hit me in the stomach game" by someone. The object of the game, of course, is for the challenger to be able to say, "See, you can't hurt me." Too many of these games teach children that they can't do anything against an adult. They are at a disadvantage, but they certainly aren't as helpless as those games may make them feel. Sports and other activities which teach a sense of physical competence are an antidote to that sense of helplessness.

Family games can provide an enjoyable way to practice responding to imaginary situations. The rest of this chapter describes some examples families have used.

What If. . .

This game which children play all the time on their own may be used to check a child's understanding of contingency plans. Children will often ask something like, "What if the car crashed right now?" Parents can introduce their concerns into the game by countering with their own "What if's."

- "What if your bicycle broke and someone offered to help you with it?"

- "What if someone took your tricycle across the street?"

- "What if I'm not home when you get home from school?"

- "What if the neighbor across the street asked you to come in and see the new kittens?"

- "What if the babysitter asks you to keep a secret?"

What ifs can be fun if everybody gets to ask questions and the children don't feel there are "right answers."

> *"Our family looks forward to playing 'What if...' games during dinner. My husband and I bring questions of sexuality and sexual assault intermittently into the conversation. For instance, I might ask, 'What if we are separated in a department store?' Followed by, 'What if someone is touching you in a way that makes you feel uncomfortable?' The children delight in asking 'What if' questions of us too. They can express their concerns in a fun kind of way, and get satisfying answers in return."*

55

"What if" games help encourage kids to rely on themselves and give them confidence in their ability to care for themselves. They are also an interesting way to find out what children know already, and what they are curious about.

Story Telling

Here is a way to provide positive examples of children acting on their own behalf and being successful, as well as to give more concrete examples of what we have been talking about.

> *"Since our daughter was young, we have made up stories to tell her. She is always in the story. The ones she listens to best are about getting lost, being afraid of the dark, being abandoned, problems with strangers. When we moved, we told her stories about moving. We've also told one about a girl who has a babysitter who keeps trying to get her to do things she doesn't want to do. The girl is really confused, but works out some things to do and finally gets some help from her parents."*

Or a story could go like this:

> *"There was a little boy who had a favorite uncle who always bought him whatever he wanted. But the uncle would scare him by hiding behind furniture and jumping out just when the little boy came along. The little boy didn't like to be scared, but he didn't know what to do. One day he asked his father if he was ever scared. His dad said that he was sometimes. The little*

boy asked how he got unafraid, 'Did you just grow up?'
Dad asked him if something was frightening him, so
the little boy told about the uncle scaring him. His dad
helped him figure out that he could ask the uncle not to
do that any more. When dad asked him if he wanted
any other help, the little boy said he'd try it himself and
would tell dad how it went.''

Personal Space

We can help children (and probably ourselves) understand
our own space needs better with a couple of games, one of
which children play all on their own, the stare game.

The *stare game* is very simple to play. Two people stare at
each other until one of them breaks eye contact and the other
one wins. Talking about how that feels and where each feels
it (in the stomach, chest, face) can identify feelings that are
clues to being challenged or uncomfortable. We can, for
example, reinforce the idea that blushing is a clue to discomfort with someone.

Another game to explore bodyspace is the *face off*. In the
simplest version, two children stand face to face, back up
from each other, and then walk toward each other until one
of them becomes uncomfortable with the closeness. Children
will goof off with this game and run into each other, but they
can tell the point at which the other is close enough. We can
emphasize the feeling of being close enough as a sign s/he
can use to protect her/himself. If this version works, then
the next step is to have the children stand side by side, then
back to back. They'll find that people can usually get much
closer without arousing discomfort.

After children have explored their own body space needs
with other children, then the same steps can be repeated
with an adult. If the children are enjoying the game, it can be
extended by pretending the adult is a stranger, then someone they know, and then someone like a parent.

These games can help children identify quickly when

someone is invading their space. They will know their own body clues and signals. By becoming quick to recognize the clues, children may later be able to react in time to keep a situation from being serious or may be able to alert an adult to the need for some help.

"No"

This game increases the likelihood that children will say "No" to an exploitative approach.

Warmup: One of the reasons that "No" isn't said more often is that rules and values may make it seem the wrong thing to do. Toddlers say no all the time, but eventually children learn not to say no. It can be fun to brainstorm with children what rules seem to encourage us to do things we might not want to do.

- "Be nice to people. It's not nice to hurt people's feelings.

- "Don't be rude. If someone speaks to you, answer him."

- "People like people who are nice, don't like people who aren't."

- "Always have to have a reason for things."

- "Take good care of your things, if someone threatens them, don't just let her take them away."

- "You are responsible for taking care of other people."

Rules like these, named, discussed and acknowledged, lose power and everybody can begin to make choices about when they want to go along with one of those rules and when it is better to say "No."

The next step then is to practice saying "No." Have two

people take turns asking favors of each other — just pretending. Practice saying "no" in different ways. When first starting this game, it works best to just say "No" and not give any reasons. As everybody gets better at a simple "No," the person asking the favor can begin saying things like, "What's the matter, don't you like me any more?" and the no-sayer can begin responding with more than "No" and see where it leads. Be sure to give children a chance to practice saying "No" to adults.

> *"I was very surprised to find that our oldest daughter couldn't say anything mean to either of us adults. Even in a mock fight game, she would sit and giggle, but she would not enter into the fight even though she would beg to play the game."*

These games can provide ways to give children practice recognizing the feelings they might have in an assault situation and to practice the responses which might get them out of the situation. As all of us work with our children to help them find ways to prevent an assault, we will discover more.

Chapter 8
How Do Kids Tell Us?

Listening

Most children do not tell in words that they have been sexually assaulted. Often the reason they don't tell is because they think no one will believe them.

> *"I told my Mom and she said she never wanted to hear talk like that again."*

Or they are afraid of what might happen, especially if the offender has threatened, "You will get in trouble if you tell" or, "You will be sent away and I'll go to jail." Children may fear that they will be blamed for the assault and that something bad will happen if they tell.

Sometimes, children may lack the vocabulary to talk about it, and don't know how to tell. They may tell in vague terms:

"I don't like Mr. Smith any more."

If they get an equally vague response, they may not say anything more. Sometimes children may think they have told, but have not been understood.

"Mr. Jones wears funny underwear."

If they've been taught always to obey their elders because grownups know what's best (and make all the rules), they may take to heart the abuser's assurances that "it's OK" or they may give promises not to tell, which they are afraid to break.

"He told me it was our special secret."

"He told me not to tell."

Usually, when children do tell about a sexual assault, some period of time has passed since the assault. Particularly if the offender is in the child's family, s/he may not tell for years.

Behavior Signals

Most often, a child will not tell in words, but by a change in behavior. Since children aren't usually able to tell someone directly, it helps to be alert to the kinds of signals a sexually assaulted child might give. For instance:

- A child may be reluctant to go to a particular place, or to be with a particular person:

  "Don't leave me alone with . . ."

  "I don't want to go with . . ."

  If a child suddenly expresses reluctance to see a favorite uncle or neighbor, or has a sudden change in play habits (afraid of school yard, church, neighbor's house), s/he is not necessarily being difficult. Children often are caught in uncomfortable situations they need help with. It is worth pursuing, especially if the suddenly disliked or feared person is one who has authority over the child.

- A child may try to express affection in inappropriate ways, such as "french kissing." S/he may show an unusual interest in the genitals of other people, or of animals, or have sexual knowledge beyond her or his age. This behavior is so startling from a small child that most adults don't know what to think.

  "There is a little girl in our neighborhood who comes to play with our children, but it is my husband that she really likes. If he is home, she wants to sit on his lap and touch and kiss him. She behaves in a very sensual way, and wants a response from him. It really blows my mind to see a preschooler act like that I'm not sure what I should do and now I'm worried about sending my kids over to her house."

One common reaction is to decide that the child has observed something s/he should not have, picked up the behavior that way and needs a reprimand. Another response may be to think that the child is simply uninhibited sexually. Both responses overlook the more likely possibility that the child has been sexually victimized and has learned the behavior from an adult or an older child.

> *"Some children at my son's nursery school were talking about how babies are made when one little girl interrupted with: 'No, that's not how mommies and daddies make babies, that's what grownups do with kids.'"*

With older children the behavior might not be as shocking because some is not quite so age-inappropriate, and it may look like seductive behavior. A child who behaves seductively is being rewarded somehow for that behavior. As s/he gets older, the reinforcement may come from peers, but in any case, sexual victimization should be suspected.

• The child may be diagnosed as having a sexually transmitted disease. If a child is diagnosed as having a venereal disease, s/he caught it from someone — either an older child or an adult. Years ago it was thought that children were uniquely susceptible to a special strain of V.D. that started spontaneously rather than from sexual contact. That is now known to be false. Somewhere in that chain of sexual contact is an adult or older child victimizing younger children.

• Other signals can include:

  - sleep disturbances (nightmares, bedwetting, trouble falling asleep, suddenly needing a nightlight)

  - not wanting to be left alone

  - irritability, crankiness

  - school difficulties (inability to concentrate)

- loss of appetite or a sudden increase in appetite

- lots of new fears, needing more reassurance, clinging

- returning to younger, more babyish behavior

- unusual behavior shift (from gregarious to withdrawn, or from easygoing to fearful)

- suddenly turning against one parent

This last group of signals are some general indicators that the child may be troubled — though not necessarily about a sexual assault. They are normal signs of upset that arise sometimes during a move, a divorce, or a new baby in the family.

Each of the "signals" identified in this chapter should be taken seriously. Parents who follow up such indicators demonstrate support for the child, and may well discover sexual approaches toward the child before a more serious situation develops.

Chapter 9
What If My Child Has Been Assaulted?

Reassuring the Child

Learning that a child has been assaulted is a crisis. It can be overwhelming. The best response is to go slowly, not ask for too much too quickly and to keep the focus on the child's needs. Reassure her/him that:

● *You are glad that s/he told you*

When the child first starts talking about the assault, s/he

can be helped by gentle questions:

"Can you tell me what happened?"

"Use your own words — it's okay to go slowly."

Don't pressure the child to talk. Ask questions that help show how the child is viewing the situation and give information back to you, for example, ask, "How were you able to tell?" rather than, "Why didn't you tell me before?" Many children feel guilty for not saying something sooner.

- *You believe what s/he has told you*

Children don't make up stories about sexual assault. Young children may have difficulty describing the incidents precisely as they occurred, complete with exact time and place. This shouldn't be a cause for disbelief. Many children who are sexually assaulted may be too young to have developed those skills. (Of one group of 583 children seen in Seattle, 58 percent were below the age of ten).

If a child is the one in five who goes back and forth between households of two natural parents, s/he may have special difficulties finding someone to believe that s/he has been assaulted by a family member. These children are often suspected of manipulation, and are sometimes denied protection because of custody and visitation issues. These children can be in intense loyalty binds and need some outside help.

- *You know it is not her/his fault*

Most kids assume the guilt for being assaulted and for causing the crisis in the family that telling about it

started. They may feel, "I did something wrong."
"I caused a lot of trouble." It's a good idea to repeat the
message that you know it's not their fault, that they are
okay.

"You didn't cause it."

"It's X's fault. He has a problem and needs help."

While making it clear that the fault lies with the offender, angry threats about what should happen to the
offender (jail, etc.) might cause a child to feel guilty
about telling. Your responses should place the blame and
responsibility with the offender in a realistic way: "What
Uncle John did was unfair. We're going to get him some
help so he doesn't hurt you or anyone else again."

● *You are sorry about what happened*

Go very slowly in assuming anything about how your
child feels. It is a good idea to keep your feelings and
reactions separate from those of your child. The child's
feelings may be completely different from your own. For
instance, your child may be very concerned about
whether the offender is going to be mad. You may be
most concerned about future sexual functioning. The
child needs to be free of your concern until hers/his is
answered.

All of us feel outrage and anger when a child has been
victimized. It's hard to focus on what the child needs
and deal with your own anger at the same time. Saying
something like, "Yes, I'm mad, but not at you" helps the
child know that s/he is not the cause of the anger.

● *You will do your best to protect and support her/him*

If the offender is a family member or a friend of the family, the child is likely to have ambivalent feelings about the offender.

The child may also be angry at the offender and want something to happen to him NOW, and not understand when there is no visible effect of having told. It's a good idea to make no promises and no threats at this point. Reassuring the child that s/he is okay, safe, and will be protected by you to the best of your abilities may help the child feel some action is being taken.

Because of the unpredictability of the medical and criminal justice system, children should not be promised anything in particular is going to happen from an exam or a police report. Often the child's trust in adults has been badly betrayed by the assault. Promising action that may or may not occur can perpetuate that sense of betrayal.

The decisions about police reporting and medical care are difficult ones. There are no "right answers." There are at least three important considerations: protecting your child from further abuse, helping your child recover from the assault, and protecting other children from the offender. Since the criminal justice system is geared toward protecting the rights of the accused, it will be up to you to do your best for your child. (In a very few areas, there are programs to assist child victim witnesses.)

The child should be included as much as possible in the process of decision making but should not be asked to make decisions which are beyond her/his ability. Choosing when to see a doctor and picking a doctor the child is comfortable with are choices in which children can be involved. They need to be allowed as much control as is reasonable without being overwhelmed by having to take responsibility for very difficult decisions. Since a child rarely relates an incident immediately after it has happened, action doesn't usually need to be taken instantly. The child may or may not be

66

ready to help with the hard decisions which need to be made until s/he has had a chance to size up adult reactions. It's okay to go slowly.

Police?

Police jurisdictions vary greatly on training and procedures for handling sexual assault of children. In most jurisdictions it is possible to back out of the proceedings. Police reporting usually involves an initial report, initial investigation, and some followup investigation. Parents may be able to assist with vocabulary, helping the child understand the police officer and helping the officer understand the child.

Ideally, the system will work so that:

- The child will be believed.

- The people involved will have some understanding and training in working with children.

- The child won't be asked to repeat indiscriminately what happened.

Exactly what happens depends on the details of the case. Each one is different. You may feel that your rights are not respected as carefully as those of the offender. Many communities have rape crisis centers which can provide specific information about the system operating in your community. They can help you throughout the process.

Medical Exam?

If your child is not physically injured, you may wonder if s/he needs a medical examination. A good medical check-up can be reassuring to your child. It should focus on your child's feelings, rather than on the genitals. In most cases, a child benefits more from being prepared to see the doctor, rather than rushing to get medical care. Children sometimes feel that a medical exam is a test, that they might pass or fail, and be okay or not okay. This is a good time to reassure your child that s/he is okay, and the purpose of the exam is to test for specific things.

You might explain in detail what will happen at the doctor's office — whether it will hurt, and why it's being done. The exam will test for different things depending on the age of the child, and the type of sexual assault. It may be necessary to test for sexually transmitted disease (VD), or the possibility of pregnancy. Evidence should be collected at this time by the medical staff to be used later if you choose to prosecute.

Your family doctor may be experienced in working with child victims, and sensitive to their needs. But some doctors are not equipped to see victims and to collect evidence. Hospital emergency rooms are an alternative. Crime victim's compensation is sometimes available from state governments to cover expenses. There are also state agencies who are responsible for investigating child abuse and neglect, including sexual abuse. Their services are intended to protect children from further abuse. In most states, any professional who believes a child is in danger of further abuse is required to contact that agency.

It is worth noting that, as this is written, the law in California (and perhaps elsewhere) *requires* physicians, social workers, psychologists, and treatment professionals of all kinds to report to the police *any* incident involving sexual assault of a person under 18. Finding out about current local laws will make the decision making process easier, should the need arise.

Chapter 10
Will Everything Be Okay After the Crisis?

"My little boy was assaulted a while back and every-thing went fine at first. He didn't seem very bothered but now I wonder how he is doing. He never brings it up, but he doesn't seem like the same spunky little boy."

How difficult the child's recovery is depends on how old the child is, how mature for her/his age, and the type of assault. The closer the offender is to the child, and the longer the assault continued, the more long-term the effects will be. Support and comfort from those close to the child and talking about it can hasten recovery.

In the past, parents were advised not to talk to the child about the assault. It was thought that not talking about it would make it easier for the child to get over it.

"I remember the way my mother reacted when I told her about the neighbor man. She held me on her lap, asked calmly what had happened and reassured me that I would be safe now. I felt guilty about how nice she was being, because I thought somehow what had happened was my fault, especially since I hadn't told anybody sooner. But weeks later when I finally asked why the police didn't do anything, I was told the police thought that little girls made things like that up, and they couldn't do anything. I thought my parents believed the police and I didn't ask anything after that. They never mentioned it again. I spent a lot of time wondering about whether or not I was all right and sometimes I even wondered if I really had made it up. I wish she had known I needed to talk about it."

The incident is not forgotten, even if it is not discussed. The more a child can talk about the experience, the more control s/he will gain over it. Talking about the experience is as therapeutic for children as it is for adults. Children benefit by expressing themselves with words, tears, drawings, dolls and puppets — whatever helps them share their experience. By talking with children we can help them understand and express feelings of fear, anger, humiliation, guilt, confusion or embarrassment, and we can reassure them that they are believed, well, loved, whole and protected. Parents can help build an understanding that what happened was not the children's fault and help them to find ways to protect themselves in the future.

Ways and Times to Talk

Talking about the offender can help a child sort out feelings of fright, anger, or numbness. For instance, if the child sees the offender, ask how s/he feels. But even if s/he doesn't, this may still be a way to get her/him talking about the assault.

> *"You said that you were afraid of Mr. X because you didn't understand how he could be so mean to you. I still wonder about that, do you?"*

- Telling someone new about the assault can provide information about how the child is feeling about whose fault it was. "Oh, no, don't tell Grandma, she won't love me anymore" is a sure sign more reassurance is needed.

> *"I'm sure Grandma would like to know, just like she wants to help when you are hurt in other ways. She certainly won't think any less of you or blame you."*

(Be sure this is so before saying it, sometimes people surprise us unpleasantly.)

- Children with sleep disturbances can be helped with a

quiet talk at bedtime about being safe and protected now. Children with nightmares can be helped to creatively change them.

> *"My little girl really surprised me the other day talking about how she had gotten rid of a nightmare created by a TV program. She had been having sit-up-in-bed crying nightmares every night. She said that she sings herself a song in which she tells the monster in the dream to sail out to sea. It seems to have worked for her, she isn't having the nightmares."*

- During a time when the child is warm, comfortable, and secure and there is enough time to finish anything which comes up, we can ask a child to tell us the story of someone who was assaulted. If just telling a story doesn't work, sometimes the suggestion that a child tell it as it would be on TV will get a story started.

- Or maybe the parent can start the story for the child. It helps to have enough information to start close enough to the truth to engage the child. Many children can't stand inaccuracies and will then begin to participate to get it "right." The goal is to engage the child without her/him feeling tricked or manipulated.

- Or we can give some clues to the child about some feelings. It is difficult for some children to express feelings, perhaps not having had any practice in doing so, or not knowing the words. Identifying the feelings as our own gives the child the option of saying: "Oh, really, well, I feel…" Some clues might be:

> *"It really makes me sad that his life was miserable, that he didn't know any better and hurt you."*

"It sure is confusing to have someone I liked so well do something that is so hard on you. I bet that is really confusing to you, too."

"It sure does make me mad that he thought he could do that."

- A child may ask how or why someone would assault a child. Parents wonder the same thing. Children may be happy with the explanation that the person is sick or has a problem, or they may want more explanation if they are older or if they knew the offender well enough to say that he didn't seem sick.

  It may be useful to talk about the difference between the way the offender sees it and the way the child sees it. That is, he may not have meant to be hurtful. The most important idea to get across to the child is that no matter what the offender thinks, it was not the child's fault, and it was hurtful.

  A child may ask what is going to happen to the offender. The answer to that question varies so enormously from community to community that we are better off trying to find out what the child is worried about rather than trying to predict what will happen. Sometimes children are concerned that the offender get help, or that something bad happen to him (like happened to them) or just that he be away where he can't hurt them anymore. More about "what happens to the offender" at the end of this chapter.

- Encourage, but don't force your child to resume her/his normal lifestyle, according to how well s/he is able to do so. The longer normal activities are avoided, the harder it is to resume them later. For instance, the child may express the stress from the assault by wanting to stay home from school. As with other illness or trauma, some rest and recovery time may be needed. If, after two weeks, there has been no progress, more than rest time is needed. If you have done all you can, more specific help may be necessary.

"I was so glad I finally talked to someone experienced in working with kids who had been assaulted. She said that what we had been going through is normal, but that it sounded like our little girl was developing a specific phobia. Then she explained methods for overcoming phobias. It's going to take a little longer than we expected, but she'll be fine."

If these clues don't start anything, it may be time to start discussing with the child your concern about her/him feeling all alone and different. Provide as many reassurances as possible that what happened to her/him happens to lots of kids, but like the chicken pox, it goes away.

If parents get very upset, angry, seem hurt or out of control, the child will learn quickly not to talk. If that has happened, the parent can explain the original upset or anger, and point out that s/he is feeling better now and would like to help. The reactions of those closest to the child are critical to her/his recovery. Every child who has been assaulted needs constant support and understanding from the immediate family. The child's ability to cope is influenced by the way s/he is treated by the people close at hand.

Family Reactions

Sexual assault is also disruptive for the rest of the family. Each family member responds differently, but there is a general pattern. No matter what form the assault took, for a few weeks afterward the family usually goes through a crisis stage that involves the emotional reaction and upset associated with learning that a child has been assaulted.

Reactions can include: trouble sleeping, feeling sick, wanting to go out and shoot the offender, blaming the child, not being able to stop thinking about the assault, guilt, anger, and grief.

For many weeks and months beyond the assault, the family goes through a lifestyle reorganization stage. It is also a time of mood swings, nightmares, sleeping difficulties, being fearful, and feeling guilt or distress over how the child is recovering. Some parents also experience an increase in fear for their children. Parents sometimes report feeling "crazy" and unsettled, even after their child has returned to normal.

Sometimes this process of family recovery includes a "resting" stage between the crisis and the lifestyle changes. This quiet spell or lull, without anything going on, can lead one to believe that the process of recovery is over, which may not be the case.

One of the most difficult feelings for parents to get over is guilt. Guilt can work its way into anger and then into blaming the child, or into depression. The pain from the hurt of a child being sexually assaulted is inevitable, but feeling guilty is not. "If only I hadn't..." is a normal reaction, perhaps serving the purpose of making us feel as though we had more control over the situation than we really did. For parents, as well as children, it is important to remember that the responsibility for the sexual assault rests on the offender. It is natural to want to blame someone — but don't blame the child or yourself. Anger at the offender may be particularly difficult to handle and sometimes leads to irrational behavior. A parent's rage or need for revenge can be particularly frightening to a child, especially since the child may think it is directed at her/him rather than at the offender. Brothers and sisters may also become upset or frightened. They may themselves have been assaulted and not talked about it.

Because sexual assault is so disruptive, parents may also need support. It is important to unburden yourself of some of

the feelings (guilt, anger, grief) both for your own sake and
so you can better support the child. Take the time to express
your feelings to someone you trust — a friend, relative,
counselor, minister, physician, or rape crisis volunteer,
instead of trying to deal with it all alone. All these reactions
are normal. Recovery comes with talking with the child, and
with time.

How Will I Know When Things Are Better?

Getting over a sexual assault is like getting over any other
trauma. At first it seems it will never pass, then the original
troubles decrease (there are fewer nightmares, less
inappropriate behavior) and one day, you realize there
hasn't been a symptom for weeks. Sometimes children who
won't talk for months about the assault, will suddenly begin
to be angry or frightened or show feelings about what
happened just about the time everything seems to be
returning to normal.

The recovery isn't smooth. The child may be better, then
have real difficulties again. This is a "normal" progression.
The setbacks are hard, but unless everything is working
against recovery, that is what they are, just setbacks.

Recovery, of course, is indicated by a decrease in the original symptoms. Typical symptoms of a child who has been
assaulted are expressed emotionally, physically, and behav-
iorally. For the first few days and weeks, a child may be very
quiet and untalkative, scared, or may be visibly upset (fid-
geting, giggly, or crying). S/he may feel sore all over, or
complain about an arm, leg, or stomach. Sleep difficulties,
wanting to sleep in the parents' bed, bedwetting, appetite
changes, and nausea are common. Also, feeling fearful,
feeling embarrassed at what her/his friends would think if
they knew, and not being able to get it out of her/his mind.

As with the family reaction, after the crisis is past there
can be a stage when the child seems to have forgotten about
everything, and wishes not to be reminded in any way. It is

most likely that the stage of reorganization and recovery is still ahead, with the possible return of many of the symptoms mentioned above (nightmares, trouble concentrating, phobias, mood swings). This is normal.

The child who was anxious, fearful and withdrawn will become less so as s/he recovers. Some children withdraw after an assault, with few other outward symptoms of disturbance. Others are more expressive so the decrease in symptoms is easier to see. Children can be assumed to be recovering when they do better in school, play comfortably with friends their own age, and show willingness to risk new behavior and to try new things.

Children recovering are able to set better boundaries for themselves, stop seductive or sexual behavior, say "no," and meet needs for contact and affection in other ways. They are able to recognize and talk about the inappropriateness of the behavior toward them, and know that the fault lies with the offender. Some ability to express the anger and unfairness suggests much progress toward recovery.

While many children recover from being sexually assaulted with the help of their families, sometimes outside intervention is called for.

About Therapy

Any one of the following are conditions which would indicate the need for outside intervention; if the child:

- won't talk

- seems to be holding something back

- has not returned to functioning normally even though a couple of months have passed

- was assaulted by a family member.

Children try to protect their parents from pain and may not talk because they are afraid that revealing a particular detail or part of the assault pattern will be too painful for their parents to handle. If the assault occurred within the family, therapy is needed for all family members. The shock and crisis of having an incestuous situation revealed is such that all family members need help and support.

What Happens to the Offender?

Our primary concern in this book is clearly with the child and the family. Nevertheless, the question of what happens to the offender is usually present at some level. Even if children don't ask, the parents probably are wondering. At first, it is typical for offenders to deny that they had anything to do with the situation. *They* didn't do it. If confronted with the facts, they may move to admitting that something happened but blame it on someone else, alcohol, drugs, or the victim. That should never shake our faith in what the child said: children do not lie about being assaulted. (*Very occasionally* they will name the wrong person for some reason.) What we can tell children, if they are hearing the offender's story from someone, is that we know the offender has to lie and we don't believe his stories.

If there is outside intervention and the offender is moved from blaming everything but himself, he will shift to the rationalization that he didn't mean to hurt anyone. Before any faith can be put in an offender's promise not to hurt someone again, he has to face up to the hurt he caused another person. Offenders do not change without specialized professional help. They are unlikely to follow through on a treatment program without legal pressure.

Why Does Someone Assault a Child?

Satisfactory answers to this question are beyond the scope of this book. Many offenders seem to pick children because they are vulnerable, and they meet either a power or sexual need. Some offenders were assaulted themselves and learned the behavior that way. Others blame alcohol or drugs. Some are apparently very immature sexually and/or seem unable to establish effective adult sexual relationships. Most seem oblivious to the problems and hurt they cause the child.

It is unknown how alcohol affects sexual assault. At least one-third of assaults involve the use of alcohol by the offender. Alcoholics are over-represented in the population of sexual offenders. It seems some offenders drink in order to get themselves "ready" (less inhibited) to commit an assault. Others offend in an alcoholic fog and deny any responsibility for their sexual or drinking behavior.

Community and legal system response to a sexual assault range from nothing happening to the offender, to a prison or institutional stay. For example, in King County, Washington (which includes Seattle and its suburban and rural areas), in 84 cases in 1979, the breakdown looked like this:

The offender was:	%
A family member	35.7
Other adult known to the child	56.0
Stranger	8.0

After being charged:	
Offender released without bail	59.5

Of the cases charged:	
Guilty plea (no trial)	73.8
Conviction	14.3
Acquittal	8.3

Of those sentenced:

Probation with counseling 51.4
Restitution 20.3
Some jail time 47.3
Other conditions (alcohol treatment, 74.5
no further contact with victim, etc.)

These numbers are at best an indication of what might happen to an offender. Children should never be promised that something will happen until after the judge has passed sentence, and even then the sentence is subject to appeal.

Fortunately, minimizing the effects of an assault on a child does not depend on what happens to the offender in most cases.

Chapter 11
Where Do We Go From Here?

The sexual assault of children affects all of us, whether or not it has happened to our own children. The following suggestions are made for those parents who are concerned about sexual assault and want to do something besides talking to their own children.

Each of us can bring the subject out into the open by talking about it. By talking openly about the sexual assault of children we can help break the trap of secrecy and shame that has caused many victims personal pain. The suggestions in this chapter are offered as steps toward that goal.

Parents Who Were Assaulted

Many parents were themselves sexually assaulted as children. Opportunities to talk about an assault, to get help and reassurance, were rarely available in the past. Most victims tried simply to forget it, and as adults are disturbed if they notice any leftover effects. Those parents may find as they try to talk to their children that they are not as effective as they want to be. Despite well-defined plans, they may never get around to talking, or if they do, they are too upset to talk calmly.

Unresolved feelings leftover from a childhood trauma must be felt, recognized and if possible reexamined from an adult perspective. This can be done through talking to someone who can be trusted to hold a confidence, not use the information in a harmful way and to listen without interfering, interpreting or telling how one "should" feel. The trust must be strong enough to allow one to reveal the shame, guilt, confusion, excitement, fear, anger, or whatever feelings are there. A dry voice, tight throat and stiff posture are signs that the feelings are still being controlled. It may help to name the offender, describe his relationship (friend, father, older brother of your best friend) and identify the force used to gain compliance.

Some of the same surfacing can result from writing about the experience. Unsent letters seem to be powerful ways of revealing feelings. A letter written but not sent to a mother or father may reveal feelings of anger or betrayal, one to an offender may show a mixture of feelings remaining.

Sometimes the leftover feelings are too powerful to handle without the help of someone experienced in working with powerful emotions. Counseling can be helpful if the counselor understands childhood sexual assault.

Jokes About Assault

Another way to help ourselves is to stand by each other. Jokes about sexual assault of children aren't very funny. Many past sexual assault victims are greatly pained when someone tells a joke which implies blame, guilt, or enjoyment on the part of a victim. The choices when a joke is told around us include: 1) Don't respond at all, and leave;

2) Deliver a tirade or lecture; 3) "Get" the other person by revealing their ignorance about matters important to them, i.e., sexuality; 4) Calmly reply with a comment that the joke isn't funny; 5) Tell your own joke which turns the tables.

All of these have been tried, each with limited success. Our advice: pick your battles — don't waste your energy on baiters, drunks, or social arguers unless you simply want to vent anger.

Protecting Other Children

> *"My brother assaulted me, now I am worried about his children."*

> *"My father assaulted me, and I don't know about my sisters. Now I worry about my own children, when their grandfather is around."*

This sense of dread and concern is sometimes covered up with the thoughts of:

> *"It happened to me and I survived, so it must not be too terrible.*

> *"He probably outgrew it, or got over it or only did it to me."*

Unfortunately what is known about sexual offenders indicates that many will continue to assault children as long as there is no outside intervention. There is no way to know for sure in any given situation because offenders who commit few assaults and do not come into contact with authorities also do not appear in studies. But the numbers of children who are being assaulted would indicate that more suspicion, not less, is valid. To help the children who are around this person: 1) Find someone to talk to without too many prejudices and biases. A husband, sister, brother-in-law, mental health counselor, or a solid friend can provide the needed help. For example, read and discuss this book together, and develop ideas that will work for you. 2) Talk to the children involved. Find out what they already know about sexual assault and let them know you will listen to them, or help them find someone who will.

Crisis Intervention

Sometimes it is found that children have already been sexually assaulted.

> *"After a training meeting on the sexual assault of children, I was talking to my young cousins to find out what vocabulary they had, when one of them told me that her daddy, my uncle-in-law, touched her there."*

> *"I suspect the child is being sexually abused, but I just don't know what to do. I don't want to interfere, or be a snoop or make things worse for the child."*

Unfortunately the system for responding to children who are being abused through sexual assault often looks as though it produces more harm than good. However a child who is being sexually abused is being deprived of the family support, nurturing and love which s/he needs. By revealing the abuse in any way, the child is asking for adult protection and if s/he does not receive it, s/he takes on an additional burden of guilt, fear and feelings of worthlessness. Even though children's feelings about situations like this change from moment to moment, intervention is usually necessary to stop the abuse. Offenders do not change without outside intervention.

A few ideas for responding when children are being sexually abused: 1) Tell someone else; 2) Contact the local agency responsible for intervening to protect the child; 3) Talk to the child to help her/him get the help needed;

4) Expect that s/he may change her/his feelings about what is going on from day to day.

Many communities have Rape Crisis Centers and Mental Health Centers which use volunteers after training them to be helpful to victims of assault. Some communities have parent aide projects to help families in which there is abuse.

Neighborhood Action

Parents can help each other and their children by providing direct support for actions taken to prevent sexual assault. Parents frequently organize to meet other problems facing their children, for example, obtaining a stop sign for a dangerous intersection, or ensuring that playground equipment meets minimum safety standards. Parents can support each other in talking about sexual assault with their children, and to meet specific neighborhood problems as they arise.

> *"My cousin's child is in trouble with the juvenile authorities. They say he assaulted a neighborhood kid."*

> *"My neighbor said that her little boy told her that a teenage boy down the street offered him comic books if he would take down his pants."*

> *"I'm sitting here listening to you talk about sexual assault and I suddenly realize why I have been so uneasy about the neighbors and their children."*

We can talk to each other about young people like this and decide on a plan of action which will get the young person some help and protect the younger children in the neighborhood: 1) Identify whether or not there is an agency which can involve the young person in treatment. Some areas have treatment programs for adolescent offenders. Some young offenders are extremely isolated and lack badly needed information. A youth counseling service *may* be able to provide the necessary help. 2) Talk to the parents of the young person to try to enlist their help for the child. 3) Talk to the younger children in the neighborhood to warn them about this particular person, using whichever tools are most appropriate. 4) Talk to the young offender (if possible) and tell him that his behavior is harmful and that you would like to see him get some help.

In a similar way, an adult in the neighborhood may suddenly appear a danger. If the children in the neighborhood spend much time with the suspicious person, talking to them may provide information about his interactions with them.

> *"He seems like a friend of yours. I don't know him very well. What is he like?" or, "He seems to spend a lot of time doing nice things for you guys."*

The children's response to these questions should give more information about the suspicion. If the children look uncomfortable and guilty talking about the person, it is probably time to consider talking to more adults in the neighborhood.

One way to do this is to bring up a book, TV show or speaker about sexual assault. In some neighborhoods inviting a Rape Crisis Center worker or police officer working block watch programs has started people working together about a common concern.

When the information gathered points to the children being victimized, talking to them again may reveal at least one child who wants to bring the incidents to a close. S/he will be glad to be approached and have some adult protection. Notifying the police may be the next step.

School Programs

Let school teachers and administrators know that accurate information on sexual assault should be part of the curriculum. Some schools have started pilot sexual assault prevention programs with great success. As a result of speaking to students at all grade levels, rape crisis workers are convinced children are eager to obtain accurate information. There may already be people in your community working on a curriculum. Your rape crisis center, school officials, or community mental health center should know. Or, you may want to obtain the curriculum guide from a project in Minnesota. (See the "Resources" section.)

> *"One of the women on our board of trustees decided that information about sexual assault should be given in the schools. She called the principals at each of her children's schools and asked if she could request a speaker. (She had exact information about how to do that.)"*

Including sexual assault information in a safety or health curriculum might also lead to some modifications in traditional "always obey adults" school regulations.

People in authority may be interviewed about their knowledge of sexual assault to be sure that they know what to do if a child reveals that s/he has been assaulted. Do they know whom to contact, and how to provide adequate care and protection for the child? If they don't, find out what agency is responsible and establish some communication between the agency and the school.

Community Action

Every community needs people actively involved in getting better treatment for victims. As with most social change, it may be difficult to break patterns of indifference. Often community response to the issue of sexual assault of children is denial that a problem exists.

> *"Sexual assault is only a problem in poor families (city slums, broken homes)."*

Once that climate is changed through articles in newspapers or magazines, or a TV or radio program, many projects are possible:

- Improvement of the Judicial System: Most judges are elected and can be questioned about their stance toward sexual assault. Letting them know people care about the issue may improve their consideration of sexual assault cases. Volunteer judicial monitoring projects in some cities have resulted in the impeachment of at least one judge and improved treatment for many victims.

- Treatment Facilities for Sexual Offenders: More money is needed for treatment programs throughout the country. Lobbying legislators and sending "letters to the editor" can help. If offenders are simply returned to their environment because there is no treatment alternative, the cycle of victimization is likely to continue.

    "I was relieved when I heard the police in our neighborhood had arrested a flasher who had been near school. When I learned that the offense was only a misdemeanor and that the flasher could collect those and ignore them like traffic tickets, and still be near my children's school, I really felt helpless — like the system has failed us somehow."

- Countering Media Portrayal of Women and Children as Victims (including child pornography and prostitution): Women Against Violence Against Women (WAVAW) is one group actively involved in ending the portrayal of violence and sexual violence against women and children, particularly as shown through the media. Other groups monitor violence in children's TV. Others lobby for reasonable treatment of sexual offenses in local newspapers. (The privacy of a victim's name may be at the newspaper's discretion.)

● Improving Community Education and Information Programs: We can all become more informed about child sexual assault by reading, of course. Ask your local library to stock important books in this field. Use this or other books as a "study guide" for a discussion group sponsored by your service club, church group, NOW chapter, or other organization.

Invite knowledgeable speakers to organizations to which you belong. Your members will become more informed, and the "experts" will learn more about community concerns.

Send for material from "model" programs in other communities. See the "Resources" section for a few suggestions.

Make this book available to teachers, community leaders, police, mental health agencies, women's centers, churches.

Suggest that groups to which you belong make prevention of sexual assault of children a group project by raising funds for local victim services, or by starting a whole new project. The active support of local women's groups is often crucial to community acceptance of the value of services provided to sexual assault victims. Find out what groups are active by watching your local newspaper. Investigate these groups to discover where your skills and energy will result in changes important to you.

The majority of changes made in the past ten years have been achieved through efforts like these. When enough of us speak out about the sexual assault of children, *we do make a difference.*

Action Suggestions for Parents

Sexual assault of children is much more common than most of us realize. It may be preventable if children have good preparation. *To provide protection and preparation,* as parents we can:

...pay careful attention to who is around our children. (Unwanted touch *may* come from someone we like and trust.)

...back up a child's right to say "No."

...encourage communication by taking seriously what our children *say.*

...take a second look at signals of potential danger.

...refuse to leave our children in the company of those we do not trust.

...include information about sexual assault when teaching about safety.

...provide specific definitions and examples of sexual assault.

...remind children that even "nice" people sometimes do mean things.

...urge children to tell us about *anybody* who causes them to be uncomfortable.

...prepare children to deal with bribes and threats, as well as possible physical force.

...virtually eliminate secrets between us and our children.

...teach children how to say "No," ask for help, and control who touches them and how.

...model self-protective and limit-setting behavior for our children.

Should it ever become necessary *to help a child recover from a sexual assault,* as parents we can:

...listen carefully and understand how children tell us.

...support the child for telling by praise, belief, sympathy, lack of blame.

...know local resources, and choose help carefully.

...provide opportunities to talk about the assault.

...provide opportunities for the entire family to go through a recovery process.

Sexual assault affects all of us, whether or not our own children are assaulted. *To help deal with this social problem,* all of us can:

...provide sympathetic care and support to those who have been victimized.

...recognize that offenders do not change without intervention.

...organize neighborhood programs to support each other's efforts to protect children.

...encourage schools to provide information about sexual assault as a problem of health and safety.

...organize community groups to support educational, treatment and law enforcement programs.

From *NO MORE SECRETS: Protecting Your Child from Sexual Assault,* by Caren Adams and Jennifer Fay, copyright 1981. Impact Publishers, Inc., San Luis Obispo, CA 93406.

Resources

"He Told Me Not To Tell" - A 30-page parent's guide for talking to children about sexual assault from which this book grew. $2.00 each, bulk rates available, King County Rape Relief, 305 So. 43rd St., Renton, WA 98055, (206) 226-5062.

"Who Do You Tell?" - 16 mm film, color, sound, (11 minutes). For children seven to twelve: Who do you tell...when you're lost...if your house catches fire...if an adult gets too close and touches you in a way you don't understand...others. Uses both animation and live footage. Purchase, $217. Motorola Teleprograms, Inc., 3710 Commercial Ave., Northbrook, IL 60062.

Seattle Rape Relief Developmental Disabilities Project. Special education curriculum on sexual exploitation, designed to teach self-protection techniques to handicapped children. Seattle Rape Relief, Developmental Disabilities Project, 1825 S. Jackson, Suite 102, Seattle, WA 98144, (206) 325-5531.

"Top Secret" by Jennifer Fay and Billie Jo Flerchinger, sexual assault information for teenagers only. A 32-page booklet. $4.00 each, bulk rates available. King County Rape Relief, 305 So. 43rd St., Renton, WA 98055.

Child Sexual Abuse Prevention Project - Curriculum manual for school districts, piloted successfully in Minneapolis public schools. Copies, $8. Cordelia Kent, CSAPP, Hennepin County Attorney's Office, 2000 Government Center, Minneapolis, MN 55487, (612) 348-8835.

Center for the Prevention of Sexual and Domestic Violence - Information to help the religious community respond to and prevent sexual and domestic violence, particularly religious concerns of victims, offenders, and families. Rev. Marie Fortune, Director, CPSDV, 1914 N. 34th, Suite 205, Seattle, WA 98103, (206) 634-1903.

Anatomically Correct Dolls - Developed by Roi Hokinson and Brenda Watson, these dolls are helping many police departments, mental health programs, district attorneys and courts during interviews of child victims. Analeka Industries, P.O. Box 141, West Linn, OR 97068 and Migima Designs, P.O. Box 70064, Eugene, OR 97401, (503) 726-5442.

"Beyond Rape: Seeking An End To Sexual Assault" - A 29-minute color 16 mm film about sexual assault (including child sexual abuse) and the work of women's groups for more than a decade to end it. Purchase price tentative, write: WCSAP, 1063 S. Capitol Way, Room 217, Olympia, WA 98501, (206) 753-4634.

"No More Secrets" - A 13-minute color 16 mm film for children eight and older. A few friends, ages eight to ten, exchange uneasy confidences about personal experiences they've had with sexual abuse. O.D.N. Productions, 74 Varick Street, Room 304, New York, NY 10013.

Books

Adams, C., Fay, J., *No Is Not Enough: Helping Teenagers Avoid Sexual Assault.* San Luis Obispo, CA: Impact Publishers, 1984.

Burgess, A.W., Groth, A.N., Holmstrom, L.L., Sgroi, S.M., *Sexual Assault of Children and Adolescents.* Lexington, MA: Lexington Books, D.C. Heath and Co., 1978.

Burgess, A.W., Holmstrom, L.L., *Rape: Crisis and Recovery,* Bowle, MD: Robert J. Brady Co., Prentice-Hall, Inc., 1979.

Dayee, Frances S., *Private Zone*, Edmonds, Washington: The Chas. Franklin
  Press, 1982.
Finkelhor, David, *Sexually Victimized Children*. New York: Free Press, 1979.
Hindman, Jan, *A Very Touching Book*. McClure-Hindman Books, P.O. Box
  208, Durkee, OR 97905, 1983.
Palmer, Pat, *Liking Myself* and *The Mouse, the Monster, and Me*.
  (Self-esteem, feelings, assertiveness for children five and up. Teacher's
  Guides available.) San Luis Obispo, CA: Impact Publishers, 1977.
Rush, Florence, *The Best Kept Secret: Sexual Abuse of Children*. Englewood
  Cliffs, NJ: Prentice-Hall, Inc., 1980.
Sanford, Linda Tschirhart, *The Silent Children: A Parent's Guide to the
  Prevention of Child Sexual Abuse*, New York: Doubleday, 1980.
Stowell, J., Dietzel, M., *My Very Own Book About Me*. Spokane Rape Crisis
  Network, North 1226 Howard, Spokane, WA 99201.
Wachter, Oralee, *No More Secrets for Me*. Boston: Little, Brown and
  Company, 1983.
Williams, Joy, *Red Flag, Green Flag People*. (Coloring book for K-4. Good,
  bad, and confusing touch; prevention of sexual assault.) Fargo, ND: Rape
  and Abuse Crisis Center, P.O. Box 1655, Fargo, ND 58107.

Services

Child Protective Services

Every state has at least one statewide agency to receive and investigate
complaints of suspected child abuse and neglect. Protective services are
intended to protect children from further abuse. Anyone can call to ask for help
for a sexually assaulted child. Look in the phone book under Department of
Children and Family Services.

Some professionals who work with children are required by law to notify
authorities of suspected child abuse and sometimes neglect. Most states
specifically require that sexual assault be reported as child abuse.

Law Enforcement

Police can provide immediate assistance and protection, take crime
reports and collect evidence for prosecution.

Rape Crisis Centers/Crisis Intervention Services

Rape relief organizations have trained volunteers available to help. They
can provide personal support, medical and legal information and accompany
the victim through medical treatment and if requested, through police
reporting procedures. Other resources may be available in some communities.
For example, local community mental health centers, crisis hotlines and
counseling agencies may be able to help.

Child Abuse and Neglect Resource Centers [CANRC]

The federal government maintains ten regional resource centers that provide training, consulting and information to public and private agencies, volunteer groups and interested citizens about the prevention and treatment of child abuse and neglect. Printed and audio-visual materials are available for loan, sometimes with a small service fee. Complete bibliographies on the subject of sexual assault of children or the film "Who Do You Tell" may be available for loan, or perhaps information about services available in your community. For information, contact the nearest CANRC:

Region I CANRC (New England States)
Judge Baker Guidance Center
295 Longwood Ave.
Boston, MA 02115
(617) 323-8390

Region II CANRC (NY, NJ, PR, VI)
College of Human Ecology
Cornell University, NVR Hall
Ithaca, NY 14853
(607) 256-7794

Region III CANRC (DE, MD, PA, VA, WV, DC)
Howard University
Institute for Urban Affairs and Research
P.O. Box 191
Washington, DC 20059
(202) 686-6770

Region IV CANRC (AL, FL, GA, KY, MS, NC, SC, TN)
Regional Institute for Social Welfare Research
P.O. Box 152
Athens, GA 30601
(404) 542-7614

Region V CANRC (IL, IN, MI, MN, OH, WI)
Graduate School of Social Work
Univ. of Wisconsin, Milwaukee
Milwaukee, WI 53201
(414) 963-4184

Region VI CANRC (AK, LA, NM, OK, TX)
Graduate School of Social Work
University of Texas at Austin
Austin, TX 78712
(512) 471-4067

Region VII CANRC (IA, KS, MO, NB)
Inst. of Child Behavior & Devel.
Univ. of Iowa, Oakdale Campus
Oakdale, IA 52319
(319) 353-4825

Region VIII CANRC (CO, UT, WY, ND, SD)
Nat. Center for the Prevention & Treatment of Child Abuse & Neglect
1204 Oneida Street
Denver, CO 80220
(303) 321-3963

Region IX CANRC (AZ, CA, HI, NV, Guam, Trust Terr. Pacific Islands, American Samoa)
Department of Special Education
California State University
5151 University Drive
Los Angeles, CA 90032
(213) 224-3283

Region X CANRC (AK, ID, OR, WA)
157 Yesler Way, Suite 208
Seattle, WA 98104
(206) 624-1062